CROWOOD EQUESTRIAN GUIDES

Basic Training

BARBARA RIPMAN

The Crowood Press

First published in 1991 by
The Crowood Press Ltd
Gipsy Lane, Swindon
Wiltshire SN2 6DQ

© The Crowood Press Ltd 1991

All rights reserved. No part of this publication may be reproduced
or transmitted in any form or by any means, electronic or
mechanical, including photocopy, recording, or any information
storage and retrieval system without permission in writing from the
publishers.

British Library Cataloguing in Publication Data
Ripman, Barbara
    Basic training
    1. Livestock. Horses. Training
    I. Title   II. Series
    636.1088

    ISBN 1 85223 534 9

Disclaimer:
Throughout this book the pronouns 'he', 'him' and 'his' have
been used inclusively and are meant to apply to both males and
females.

Acknowledgements:
All photographs by Louis Milburn.
All line drawings by Hazel Morgan.

Typeset by Footnote Graphics, Warminster, Wiltshire
Printed in Great Britain by BPCC Hazell Books, Aylesbury

CONTENTS

Young people of today have achieved many successes in the equestrian field. They show a lot of natural ability, sometimes with a minimum of guidance from others, acting purely on the instinct to apply themselves in a simple, uncomplicated manner.

Not all riders have this exceptional talent and the aim of this book is to assist these riders by shedding more light on an immense subject, enabling them to proceed with more knowledge and awareness of the basic requirements of training the horse.

Even if at first they are not successful, they must never tire of trying as they will achieve great satisfaction from a job well done. The use of gadgets to take short cuts will only produce an artificial result and a false pride.

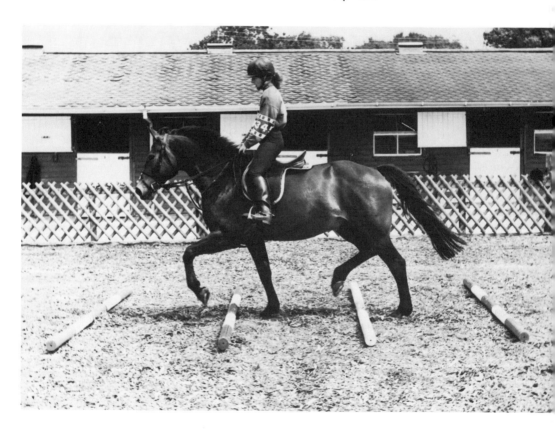

When undertaking the schooling of a horse, the rider must have considerable experience in equestrian skills; it is not possible to teach another, whether human or animal, if you lack knowledge yourself. It is even possible to have a lifetime's experience of riding but still lack the necessary skills to train and school a horse. However, for those who do undertake the task, it is both absorbing and fulfilling.

It would be wrong, even foolish, for the trainer to assume that a horse lacks intelligence; quite often the horse will learn the faults of the rider more quickly than the rider can learn those of the horse. Apart from practical ability, it is also beneficial to have an understanding of horse psychology. He is by nature a herd animal who, in general terms, accepts the leader of that herd as his master. So once placed in a domesticated environment, the trainer must take over this master/leader position. When the horse's education is carried out by such a trainer, with both mental and physical abilities, it is possible to produce a horse schooled to a level that makes him a pleasurable and obedient ride.

This book's aim will be to give the young and inexperienced trainer some guidelines to follow when undertaking the training of the young or uneducated horse. Obviously, nobody is perfect, and mistakes will probably be made in the initial period, but provided an open mind is kept, these mistakes can be rectified, and the experience gained invaluable.

Before proceeding with mounted work, it is beneficial for the trainer to observe the horse's attitudes in and around the stable. First, look at his general response to human contact and his immediate surroundings, whether he shows confidence or nervousness, or even sometimes putting up forms of defence like kicking or biting. Time must be taken to understand these habits and to gain the confidence and trust needed before serious training can commence.

These days, the trainer is quite often the groom as well, and so deals with the daily welfare of the horse around the stable. In these circumstances it is possible to observe the horse's behaviour patterns throughout the day, rather than just during schooling sessions. Some of the first requests to be made of the horse are those asked of him by the groom in the stable, and it is vital that they be made in a quiet but firm manner and the horse praised with voice or touch. This will form a basic understanding by the horse of the approach and attitude of his trainer.

Horses, like people, show many varieties of temperament and behaviour patterns, and the trainer must decide on the best approach for each individual. With some, a strong, dominating attitude is required, but with a more nervous, highly-strung type, a quiet, steady approach must be adopted. With the progression of the training programme, it will be found that the behaviour patterns change and the personality develops according to the influence of the trainer.

It is quite probable that horses are not the trainer's primary occupation, but a secondary one that must fit in around his main job. However, it should not be forgotten that schooling a horse necessitates spending regular periods working with him, as it is only through repetition at regular intervals that the horse learns. When putting time aside for this daily job, always allow a little longer than you think will be necessary, as it is often when limited by time that things go wrong, or that the horse has a problem which must be resolved there and then. From the start try to make the training sessions varied and enjoyable, never asking more than you think the horse is capable of giving at that time.

(*Right and opposite*) The same horse before training has commenced and again two years later. The photographs show how good work can develop a horse in the right places.

Sometimes a new horse is purchased to be trained on for a specific job, or the trainer undertakes the further education of an older horse which he feels could be improved by correct riding techniques. If you are considering the purchase of a horse, then a few points must be taken into account.

TEMPERAMENT

A very important point – a horse can always be influenced by good handling, but can seldom be totally changed. It is therefore something that the new owner might have to live with for a very long time, and so it is better to start with the right sort of temperament and one you feel you can get along with.

SIZE AND PHYSIQUE

This should be thought of in relation to the size and physique of the rider, and must be such that they feel compatible. It is not

(*Above and right*) The same horse trotting loose in an arena showing how appearance can differ between an engaged and active horse and one who is lacking concentration and has a lazy stride.

advisable to start training a horse that is able to prove that he is bigger and stronger than his rider. If the horse is to be a show horse, then he should be measured to ensure that he falls within the height required for that class.

MOVEMENT

This is a basic requirement more of the show and dressage horse than of the jumper. When a horse is able to execute all three paces in a correct manner, he can then be classed as having good movement. He does not need to be extravagant to be good, although this can be very eye-catching. The type of movement must, however, be suitable for the job required. If the horse shows limitation in movement, it is necessary to decide whether or not good riding/training can correct this or not in order to avoid wasting time.

CONFORMATION

This is again more important to the show and dressage horse than to the jumper, but a good shape must be a requisite of a good athlete. Correct work can help build the young or under-developed horse into a better outline by developing specific muscle groups for particular jobs. This can influence the final shape and appearance of a horse, and so change his conformation.

If the horse matches up to the requirements of the trainer in all these ways, he should then be vetted to ensure he is sound in health and movement. It would be silly to undertake years of schooling with a horse that is not initially sound.

At the end of this preliminary training period, it should be possible to ascertain whether the horse will be able to perform the task the trainer has in mind, and to have produced a horse that is a pleasant and co-operative ride.

When taking on a new horse and putting him into a new environment, it is important to give him a 'settling in' period. The trainer will have an opportunity during this time to cover some of the basic ground work and to get to know his horse, gaining its confidence at the same time. The older horse might well be established in some of this basic work, but it should still be an opportunity to get to know and understand each other.

If possible, try to find out as much as you can about any previous training the horse might have received, as this might influence your approach to him. Not all young horses have received a good start – some of the training might have been rushed or even totally overlooked. It does not do any harm in such cases to run through the basics again and do the job properly, as taking short cuts now may well give rise to problems later on.

Horse standing square for showing.

Much of this basic work can be done in and around the stable, where the trainer can accustom the horse to his ways and manners. He must learn confidence in, for instance, being touched and stroked all over, or being tied up to a ring in the stable (best done initially via a piece of string for safety). When he will stand quietly tied up in this manner, he can then get used to being groomed and manoeuvred around the stable, moving to left and right when touched on one side and asked at the same time with the voice. He should become accustomed to having his legs and feet touched and lifted until he will do this easily when asked by touch and voice.

Even in these simple tasks, observe how quickly he settles and obliges to these requests, and how he adjusts to his new environment and routine, as it will give an insight into how he might respond to other situations in the future.

It is important that the horse is content in his new stable, as,

Horse standing square for dressage.

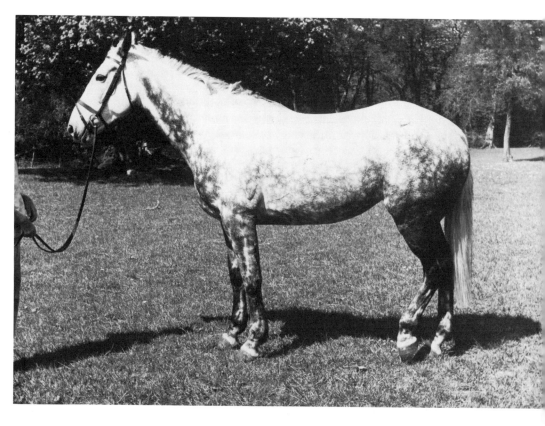

Horse standing incorrectly and lazily.

if he is relaxed, he will 'look' well and 'do' well. The stable must become the horse's haven, where he can switch off from outside pressures, but he should look forward to visitors entering his stable, and turn to approach them with confidence and curiosity. If he shows fear or nervousness in these situations, then time and patience must be spent to gain his trust until he ceases to look on people as a threat.

With a normally adjusted horse, it only takes a few days to form this basic contact, and to get him to carry out simple requests. He can then be taught to lead out in hand correctly; this means he must willingly keep up with his trainer, halt when asked, and learn to stand square. Again, sometimes the older horse has no idea how to carry out this simple exercise, because it has been omitted from his early training.

Patience must be shown to teach the horse to stand square, as he should not be permitted to stand in a lazy or idle manner.

The trainer must first insist that he places weight on all four legs without resting one of them, and he should be praised and encouraged when this is achieved. From this position he must be taught to stand either four-square as a dressage horse, or, if a show horse, with all four legs placed so they can be seen (*see* pages 10–11). If he persists in resting a particular leg, then the leg must be tapped with a whip to make him stand up on it, so explaining what is required, and give praise when it is achieved.

Leading is best done with a snaffle bridle, the reins taken

A horse being led correctly and well-positioned to the leader.

over the head and held firmly for control. The right hand holds the reins about 6–8in (15–20cm) below the bit rings with the first finger placed between the reins to separate them. The left hand then holds them about 18in (45cm) below the right nearer the buckle end (*see* page 13). The trainer then turns in the direction he wants to go and, keeping about level with the horse's shoulder, gives the voice command 'Walk on', and at the same time, starts to walk forward and encourage the horse to keep up with him. The trainer should carry a whip to use as assistance if the horse is reluctant to walk. This should be carried in the left hand, pointing down and back. Again the command 'Walk on' is given, and if he is still reluctant to move, a light tap on his flank should be given with the whip to make him step forward with the leader. When he is then asked to halt, the voice command should be combined with a restraining feel on the reins, and the horse brought to a standstill.

Repeat this walk/halt sequence a few times, until he realizes what is expected. Progression is made by then proceeding to the trot using the voice and touch aids to encourage the horse to stay alongside the leader. Then by the same means he is

(*Right and opposite*)
Showing how, if the leader falls too far behind the shoulder of the horse, the horse shoots forward and the leader is in a dangerous position.

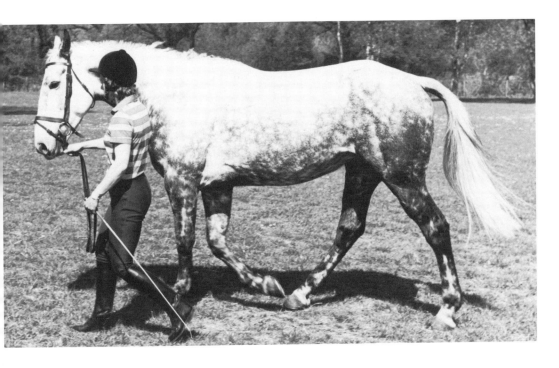

asked to walk and return to halt when asked. The objective of these exercises is to teach the horse to associate voice (sound) and action; for this reason, it is important to give the voice command in the same tone of voice, so that there is no confusion over its meaning. If these simple tasks are performed well, then reward must be given, especially with a nervous horse. Even small titbits are allowed in order to gain trust and confidence.

The leader must never be too far back from the horse's shoulder, especially when trotting, as this can be very dangerous should the horse shoot forward and kick or buck. The trainer could find himself directly in the line of fire from the back legs.

At the end of these sessions, he should be enthusiastic about keeping up with the trainer, but stop and stand when asked without getting too strong or trying to stop before being asked.

Whilst getting to know your horse around the stable, it is a good time to fit him with rugs, rollers, bridle and saddle, making sure they all fit snugly. In fact, the more handling and contact between horse and trainer at this stage, the better and quicker trust will develop and progress be made.

The following is a list of the necessary equipment, with instructions for fitting.

BRIDLE

Adjust bit to the correct height where it will fit snugly into the corner of the lips. If too high, it will cause discomfort, and if too low could touch the incisor teeth. It is also possible for a horse to put his tongue over a low bit which is a difficult habit to break.

The browband should not be too short, as it will pull the headpiece forward and cause pressure at the back of the ears. The throatlash should not be too tight, as it will hinder and cause discomfort when flexion is required.

The bit positioned too low.

The bit positioned too high.

NOSEBANDS

Drop Fits below the bit and closes the mouth by being buckled fairly tightly around the mouth. Should not drop too low over the nostrils as this can impair breathing.

Cavesson This should be adjusted in length so that it sits about ¾–1in (2–2½cm) below the facial cheekbones, and should be of a size that can be made tight around the jaw if necessary. This can help prevent the jaws crossing and opening.

Flash Combination of the two above, the cavesson part should sit level and be tight, the bottom strap fits below the bit and is done up comfortably but firmly.

Correct fitting of a drop noseband.

Correct fitting of a cavesson noseband.

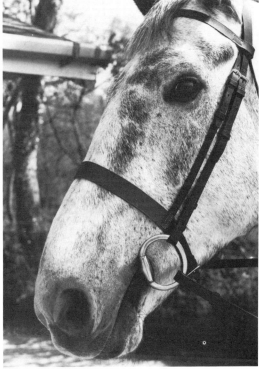

Correct fitting of a flash
noseband.

Correct fitting of a grakle
noseband.

Grakle or Figure 8   Similar to the flash, but the design forms more of a 'X' than the flash. If the two straps slide through a pad on the top of the nose, the action is such that if the horse tries to open his mouth, it tightens around the jaw; if he resists in the jaw, it will tighten around the mouth.

The trainer must decide which of these is most suitable for each individual.

BITS

A snaffle should be used for all basic training, but there are a large selection to choose from; straight bar, double jointed,

loose ring single joint
metal or rubber

eggbut single joint
metal or rubber

loose ring French
link mouthpiece

T-cheek loose ring
single joint

straight bar (mullen mouth)
can be metal or vulcanite

T-bar French link

D-ring snaffle
metal or rubber coated

rubber straight bar
loose ring

eggbut French link

A selection of snaffle bits with a variety of mouth and cheek pieces.

single jointed, each with a different ring or cheekpiece or of different thicknesses (*see* above). It should be wide enough to prevent rubbing in the corners of the lips. If it is too wide, it can lose its correct action; ideally it should protrude out of the corners of the mouth about ½in (1½cm) on both sides. Sometimes a loose ring can cause the lip corners to become sore, when an eggbutt is probably better.

LUNGE CAVESSON

Fits slightly lower than the cavesson noseband. Both top and bottom straps must be done up firmly, otherwise it will twist around the head during work, and the cheek pieces can catch the horse near or in the eye. The snaffle bridle is fitted underneath, and the noseband is not necessary if the cavesson is fitted properly.

The bit too wide for the mouth.

LUNGE ROLLER OR SURCINGLE

Ideal for lungeing, as it is purpose-made for the job with 'D's and rings in the correct places for side reins etc. Place a small pad under the top arch to prevent pressure on the spine. Girth up firmly to prevent it rolling, as this can cause rubbing.

SIDE REINS

Ideally use leather reins, but webbing ones are fine though these should preferably be without elastic inserts as this can encourage the horse to yank and pull at the rein contact. Both reins should be fitted to the same length. Initially they should be kept long so as not to pull the horse's head into its body, forming a restricted shape. They should not be clipped to the bit rings until the horse has been led to the exercise area and has commenced work. Only in exceptional circumstances should the inside rein ever be taken shorter than the outside.

LUNGE LINE

Best made of thick cotton webbing, as nylons and synthetics can cause burning if they are pulled through the trainer's hand by a strong horse. The line should be as long as possible at least 30 feet (10 metres) long to enable the horse to stay on a large circle. Attach it to the centre ring of the cavesson.

An incorrectly fitting saddle. The front is too high and the back too low. It would place the rider's weight too far back and tilt him backwards.

SADDLE

For the novice horse, a general purpose saddle is the most suitable, as stirrups need not be too long for all-round riding. The saddle must be a good balanced fit, not sloping down or up, but having a level appearance when viewed from the side. There should be good clearance over the wither and along the spine. The pads to each side of the spine should be wide and flat for good weight distribution. If the front arch is too narrow, it will sit the front of the saddle up too high, causing it to slant backwards and so tilt the rider in the same way. A cotton or sheepskin numnah or saddle pad is ideal, and should be large enough to slightly protrude all around the saddle. Synthetics can sometimes cause skin problems.

EXERCISE BOOTS

Very beneficial to the horse when being ridden or lunged, giving the legs protection from knocks from another leg or foot. The velcro fastening types are more than adequate.

BANDAGES

These will give good support, but care should be taken when putting them on, as a lot of damage can be caused if applied by an inexperienced person. They must be firm enough to

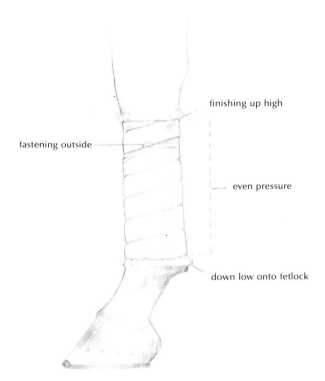

finishing up high

fastening outside

even pressure

down low onto fetlock

Exercise bandage for a foreleg, giving support during work.

The running martingale and standing martingale can assist the rider in lowering the horse's head carriage.

port, with an even pressure throughout, but not be too tight. On the other hand if they are too loose, they can be useless or dangerous to the horse. Ideally, they should be long enough to start below the knee and cover right down the tendons, then return finishing again at the top.

RUNNING MARTINGALE

This can occasionally be useful with a young horse or an older one that perhaps lacks control in faster paces or jumping, because it can limit the upward movement of the head and neck. It must not be adjusted too tightly, affecting the head and neck when they are carried in correct posture, but should only come into operation when the head and neck are raised. The reins should be fitted with reins stops to prevent the rings of the martingale being caught on the buckles.

STANDING MARTINGALE

Not often used, but in rare cases it can be a help with an older horse with a long-standing problem of carrying the head and neck too high. It is attached from the girth to the noseband to hold the head in a restricted downward position.

Artificial Aids

A whip should always be carried to assist leg aids.

Spurs should not substitute for leg aids, but they can be useful to assist the leg. The horse must never be abused or punished with them.

Lungeing can be beneficial to both the young and the older horse, helping to improve such things as balance, obedience, relaxation, suppleness with forward movement in a correct outline and a calm acceptance of the bit. There is no reason why this work cannot be carried out in conjunction with everyday riding, as lungeing can only help improve the ridden work. With the right preparation and equipment, there is no reason why any horse cannot be lunged reasonably correctly, and for it to prove advantageous. Occasionally, because of a physical problem, a veterinary surgeon might advise against it, and this advice should be heeded.

Prior to putting the horse on the lunge and expecting him to make a correct circle around you, as the hub, he can be given an introduction by teaching him to parallel lead. This is an extension of leading and the horse and trainer move forward together in parallel lines approximately 6–8ft (1–1½m) apart. This can be done both in walk and trot quite easily with the trainer and the horse level in a parallel line. This preparation for lungeing is quite easy to learn, and can be helpful to the trainer who has to work without an assistant.

First equip the horse as for lungeing, fitting the bridle with the lunge cavesson over the top, then attaching the lunge line to the centre ring. A saddle or roller can be used with side reins attached, adjusted so they are the same length. The most important thing is that they should be long enough to allow the horse to extend the neck and head, but be clipped back on the 'D's of the saddle or roller until work has commenced.

Hold the lunge line with the right hand, about 18in (45cm) from the cavesson, with the rest of the line taken up into loops of approximately 14–16in (35–40cm) in size, and held firmly in the left hand. Instead of a schooling whip, a lunge whip must now be carried in the left hand pointing down and back.

Lead the horse forward as before in walk and trot to familiarize him with the new equipment he is wearing. If this is accepted with no problems, then the side reins can be attached to the bit rings.

Proceed again into walk, and start to allow the horse a little more length of line to create a wider gap between him and you, but instead of standing still, continue to walk with the horse, staying about level with his shoulder. To save taking as much exercise as the horse, gradually bring him onto a large (approximately 90ft or 30m) circle.

Right hand showing how to hold the rein when about to lunge on the right rein.

to horse

Correctly looped lunge line. When lungeing commences the hand must be firmly shut.

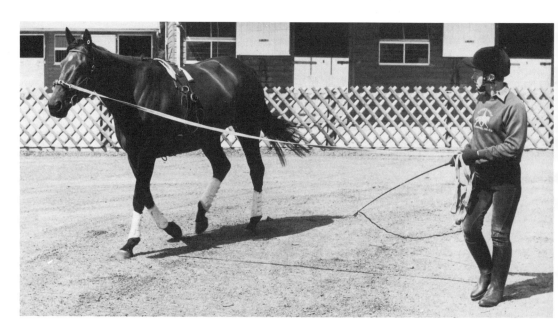

The horse and trainer correctly placed for parallel leading in walk.

Maintain forward movement with the voice and whip, now carried in the right hand pointing low and towards the hind quarters. Carry the lunge line in the left hand at about waist height.

The horse learns to work confidently and well in this manner at all paces. With the trot and canter, it is necessary for the trainer to walk faster on the smaller circle so as to stay parallel to the horse's shoulder, but still maintaining the 6–8ft (2–2.5m) gap. When the horse increases pace, it is important not to be left behind, because if the horse gets ahead of the trainer, it can place him in a dangerous position, level with the back legs instead of the shoulder.

Using this exercise, it is possible to teach the horse to keep the lunge line taut, and prevent him dropping its contact and avoiding work on the circle. The feel down the lunge line should eventually become an extension of the hand feel, and be the same as that required on the riding rein. Parallel leading can prevent the development of bad lungeing habits, the worst of these being the habit of cutting in across half the circle and pulling away on the other. It can also be dangerous if the horse dives into the circle, the lunge line goes slack, and becomes entangled around his legs. In such cases, control is lost and it is possible for the horse to break away from the trainer.

The horse and trainer correctly placed for parallel leading in trot.

When moving on a circle, it is necessary for the horse to slightly bend to the curve of the circle. A steady restraint should be put on the line to lead the horse's head towards the circle, and as he turns his head to the required direction the line is lightened to show him he has done the correct thing.

Try not to let the contact on the lunge line become a strong steady pull, as this will encourage the horse to do the same, ending up with a tug-of-war situation which the horse will win.

When the horse is required to slow down or stop, the feel down the line should explain what is needed. From the quiet leading and yielding action, the hand must take stronger, intermittent contact and, with the combination of the voice, he will quickly learn what is required. Because of the closeness of horse and trainer during this exercise, the aids from the hand are much more influential on the shorter rein, and it is possible to maintain better control and concentration.

When sufficient obedience has been learned on this short rein, he can then be allowed to move out onto the longer rein until the full lunge circle is used with the same control.

Over the years, I have used parallel leading with many horses as an introduction to lungeing, and have found it a very advantageous and simple way of teaching horses to lunge.

It is necessary to decide where you are going to carry out the lunge exercise, and do any preliminary work. A trainer can give himself a lot of trouble by taking a horse to the middle of a field, without any assistance, and expecting it to simply go around in circles. The usual result is to lose control of the horse, and the efforts of the trainer proving totally inadequate.

Not everybody has the advantage of an outdoor or indoor schooling area, suitably fenced and with safe footing, and many have to make do with the facilities they have. However, with a little forethought, it is possible to make temporary provision to enable the job to be done adequately.

Those with an indoor or outdoor facility can have an advantage especially in bad weather. However, it is still necessary to divide off an area of about 60x60ft (20x20m), which is ideal for lungeing on the circle.

If either horse or trainer lack experience in the art of lungeing, it can be a help to build a temporary enclosure around the square to be used. This only needs to be of simple construction, using jump poles and stands, or any other similar material which is easily to hand. Just the sight or feel of an enclosure is enough with some horses to confine them to the required area, and once control is established the enclosure can be dispensed with.

Surfaces

The trainer should check that the ground conditions are suitable for the job. A valuable horse can easily be ruined if worked on a surface that could cause strain or injury.

Do not lunge near hazards of any kind.

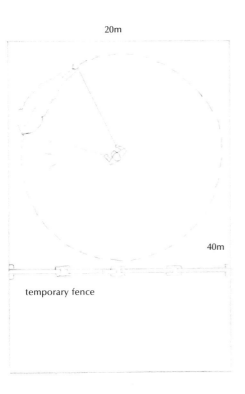

20m

40m

temporary fence

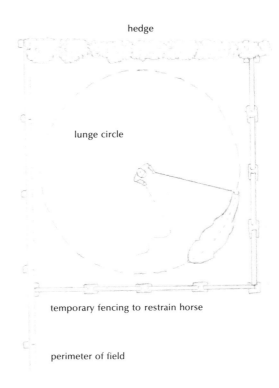

hedge

lunge circle

temporary fencing to restrain horse

perimeter of field

Those who only have a field to work in should always think of using one of the corners, as this will give you two sides of your perimeter fence. The other two sides can be temporarily fenced in the same manner with jump poles, stands etc. Even with the fairly well-behaved horse, greater concentration can be maintained when he is confined in this way.

It is *very important* not to lunge near wire fences or ditches or any sort of hazard. Even the quietest horse can take fright and get out of control. On all occasions, ensure gates, doors etc. are closed and fastened.

One advantage of training horses outside is that once concentration has been learned with all sorts of distractions going on around them, they are quicker to settle in strange surroundings than the horse that has been confined to an indoor arena. Those horses sometimes take a while to re-adjust to working in the open on uneven ground. Sometimes the horse is so unused to working outside that a lot of the first basic schooling has to be covered again to settle him.

(*Left*) An indoor or outdoor arena, and (*right*) using the corner of a field to provide two fences. Temporary fencing can assist the lunger in restraining a wayward horse.

Objectives of Lungeing

To teach obedience and trust.
To help balance.
To learn to travel to left and right.
To develop physique.
To improve rhythm and tempo.

Lungeing is truly an art, and can be a tremendous help in producing an obedient, balanced horse who will move to both left and right before being asked to do this with the weight of the rider. The progression from the previous work to lungeing should be easy, but remember, its main purpose is to educate the horse.

A lunge session should proceed as follows: equip the horse with a bridle and lunge cavesson over the top with lunge line attached to the centre ring. Fit the saddle and numnah with a surcingle over the top to stop the flaps lifting and banging. Attach side reins to the girth straps under the saddle flaps, not too low, but make them equal in length and start with them very long. At this stage, leave them clipped back to the saddle. Do not forget boots or bandages for protection or support.

Lead the horse to the lunge area and onto the perimeter of the lunge circle, facing the direction he should go. Most horses find the left-handed circle the easier one to start with. Halt the horse, and attach the side reins to the bit rings, but make sure they do not restrict the natural length of the neck. Pulling in the head and shortening the neck artificially can have long-lasting effects on a horse, and create a problem which is difficult to correct later on.

Start the lungeing with a little parallel leading, but going straight into a large circle, where he should walk with confidence. Once he has settled and is walking with energetic strides, gradually lengthen the lunge line, stepping back away from the horse, until he is walking in a large circle independent of the trainer, who must then take up a position in the centre.

If the previous exercise has been practised well, it should be possible to keep a taut lunge line. To prevent the line getting too low, and to help keep control, the trainer's hand which is holding the line must be kept at least at waist height, and the arm bent at the elbow. It is also necessary to adopt a square stance which is strong and firm. The other hand holds the lunge whip, carried about 2–3ft (½–1m) above ground level, pointing towards the rear of the horse.

Again, voice commands are used, supported by the whip to keep the horse moving forward. If any major problems are encountered, do not chase and frighten the horse, but have an assistant help by leading him forward until he gets the right idea. Once achieved, the assistant can step aside and let the horse continue alone.

As the horse understands what is required and is more confident, he can be put forward into trot, asked for by the voice and enforced by showing the whip. The trot strides must be energetic and regular, in order to begin to develop the rhythm and balance that must eventually become habit. Whilst in the trot, he must be encouraged to bend to the direction of the circle. This is achieved by taking a restraining action on the line to turn the head and neck towards the circle. The trainer should think of this as leading the horse's head and neck forward and into the circle, and as he obliges, should lighten the feel to show him he has done the job well. This intermittent feel can be taken as frequently as necessary to achieve the aim of curving him to the perimeter of the circle.

When he is required to reduce pace or stop, the voice command is given again, with shorter, stronger feels on the line. Keep the lunge whip down and away from the horse, and the voice tone should be quiet and drawn out. With any small achievement, praise must be given. Once a few transitions have been made, he can be stopped and turned to the other direction, and the same tasks performed to this rein. The

The stance of the trainer while lungeing is important in order to keep control of the horse.

transitions from halt to walk, trot and down again should be practised until he is confident and is finding it easy to both reins, then the canter can be attempted.

To attempt the canter on the lunge, the trainer should be sure that the horse is working in a more balanced manner in walk and trot. If the canter is attempted before this, because he may feel he is losing balance, he could well shoot off at speed in an effort to try and regain it. This will only create fear and apprehension for both horse and trainer, and a reluctance to try again. For some, balance in the canter is very easy, and hence presents few problems. For others, it can prove more difficult and will only be achieved with the enthusiasm and insistence of the trainer. In such cases, the lunge line should increase the action of leading the head and neck forward and into the circle, at the same time a strong voice command given, followed through with the action of the whip to create the canter. Initially, it is sometimes necessary to give the commands in this strong way to impress on the horse what he must do. Immediately he responds, a soothing, quiet voice should be used to dispel any worry or fear, but it should be stimulating enough to try and maintain the canter pace.

Trainer correct to horse.

Lunger in correct and safe position to horse.

Only try to maintain the canter pace for short periods in the beginning, as it is unlikely that he will be able to cope with more than one or two circuits, and so ask him to return to trot before he tries to break himself.

Occasionally, through freshness or excitement, he might break into the canter on his own. Never discourage this, but praise with the voice and urge him to continue for a few circuits before asking him to return to trot. When this attitude is adopted, the horse quickly learns to enjoy the canter, and it can become part of the daily work.

Once the canter has been performed to both reins in the same way as the walk and trot, progression can be made to more concentrated work. In this, the trainer must be able to observe that the horse is working to the best of his ability for that stage of development. He must be encouraged to put energy into his strides at all paces, and to maintain regular rhythm, and subsequently develop more swing and energy to his movement. Transitions through the paces can be carried out more frequently, thus improving the horse's balance and obedience to the voice. As the work progresses, the side reins can be shortened, one hole at a time, as the horse learns to

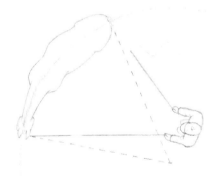

Trainer too much to the rear of horse.

Lunger too far to the rear of the horse if he should kick out or buck.

Lunge Work can Cover:

1. Improvement of head and neck position.
2. Teaching balance through upward and downward transitions.
3. Helping to lengthen and shorten both outline and strides.
4. Producing suppleness and bend around the circle.
5. Giving the horse an understanding of communication and aids.

work into an easy contact on the rein. With this slightly shorter, rounded outline, the horse's top line will start to take shape with the resultant development of the muscles along the top of his neck and over his loins and quarters. With the development of these important muscle groups, the horse will become stronger and more capable of carrying out his work in an easy manner.

This work can be combined with a simple riding routine, with the lungeing taking up about thirty per cent of the exercise programme. By combining these two forms of exercise, one can complement the other; for example, once the horse is working fairly well on the lunge, the side reins can be slightly shortened, taking the horse into a shorter, more collected outline. This will help him develop his muscles for this type of work without having to carry the rider, and will give him an introduction to a more advanced shape. This approach with the older horse can be very beneficial, especially with those that lacked schooling in their earlier years. Lungeing will teach them the correct carriage and balance needed to work on the circle, and if the driving aids of voice and whip are used efficiently, they will have the effect of driving the horse to the contact of the bit by engagement of the hind legs. Because of the balanced, stabilizing support of the side reins, forward movement is never discouraged by a backward feel being taken on the reins. This means that the horse will be enthusiastic about this forward work.

Contact down the lunge line should be developed and refined so that it becomes an extension of the riding rein, and the feels given down that rein are of the same sensitivity, producing a horse that is light and responsive in the hand.

Initially, the lunge work sessions will last approximately 15–20 minutes. If they were longer, they would prove too tiring, the muscles becoming sore and stiff because of the unfamiliar work. With the development of physique and ability, these sessions can be extended to approximately 30–35 minutes, which is normally long enough, because over-working on the lunge becomes tedious and little enthusiasm will be shown.

With the excitable or nervous horse, more time must be given to learn each new exercise, and patience must be shown with this type of horse before advancement is made.

Regularity of lungeing is important, and as with all training it is the only way that the horse learns his lessons well. It can

become a very absorbing form of training, and to lunge a well-schooled horse can be a delight.

Lunge work can include a variety of work, from collection to extension, and at the same time the trainer is able to observe whether the movement is correct. The lunge session should always be finished on a good note, and an extra five minutes should be spent letting the horse work in a long outline with the side reins unclipped to let him relax and stretch.

When brought to a halt, the trainer should always approach the horse while he remains on the perimeter of the circle. The lunge line should again be taken back into loops to stop it dragging on the ground, and the lunge whip be placed under the arm, pointing back away from the horse. Praise should be given freely as reward for his work and efforts.

A horse working on the lunge in a good outline at an active trot with side reins long and light at this stage.

A Good Position

1. Body posture should be tall and erect but not stiff and tense.
2. Head should be held high without tilt.
3. Stretched, long legs should keep contact with the horse through as much of their length as possible.
4. The heels should be lower than the toes.
5. Arms should hang in a natural position from the shoulders with elbows bent.
6. Hands should be kept closed but carried in a relaxed manner and not loose or slack.

As we have already said, the main requirement of a horse trainer is to be a good and experienced rider. This does not just mean being able to cope with and rough-ride a difficult horse, but to understand a horse's psychology, and be able to adjust his riding techniques to suit the individual.

A rider of this calibre should have a correct, balanced seat from which to transmit the aids in a clear and uncomplicated way. The individual's personal physique will affect the riding posture, but whatever the rider's make and shape, two things are extremely important to the basic balance. First, in the correct position, and viewed from the side, it should be possible to draw a vertical line from the point of the shoulder, down through the seat bones to the heels. In this position, balance can be maintained in the upright position. Second, when viewed from the front or back, the position should be equal to the left and right of the horse. A vertical line drawn through the centre of the rider should continue through the centre of the horse.

An experienced rider should have good powers of thought and concentration – if he expects concentration from his horse he must first practise it himself. Over years of riding, a rider who might have started with a good position may develop bad habits. These can produce a weak, ineffective position which is of no help in the correct schooling of the horse, as the work demands the discipline of both horse and rider. A good rider should be able to keep balance and posture at all times, through all paces, transitions, turns and circles. This will enable the horse to carry himself more easily and to maintain energetic steps, because a balanced load is an easy one.

In riding turns and circles, the rider should not slip or tilt to inside or outside, but should remain upright, equally to left and right of the horse to help him stay upright throughout.

On the circle, he should sit square to the axis; if an imaginary line was radiated from the centre of the circle, like the spoke of a wheel, it should pass through one point of the shoulder and out through the other. This also applies to the hips.

When riding a novice or unbalanced horse, the rider should not use stirrups that are too long, as this can cause a lack of balance, and also weaken the effectiveness of the aids. If a comfortable length is used, it enables the rider to give the horse as much assistance as possible.

Correct riding position from the side.

When watching an experienced rider, it is difficult for the onlooker to perceive the actions and aids given, as communications are refined and given with feel and weight distribution. The rider appears as one with the horse, and in total harmony. However, the trainer must always keep an open mind to new methods and techniques, having a desire to improve and expand his knowledge in this vast subject.

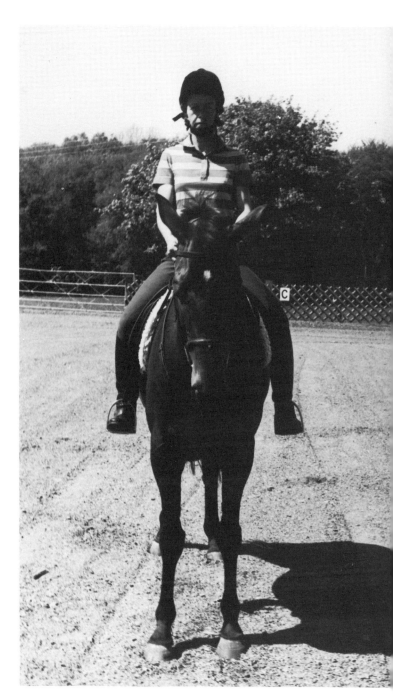

Correct riding position from the front at halt. The rider is sitting equal to left and right.

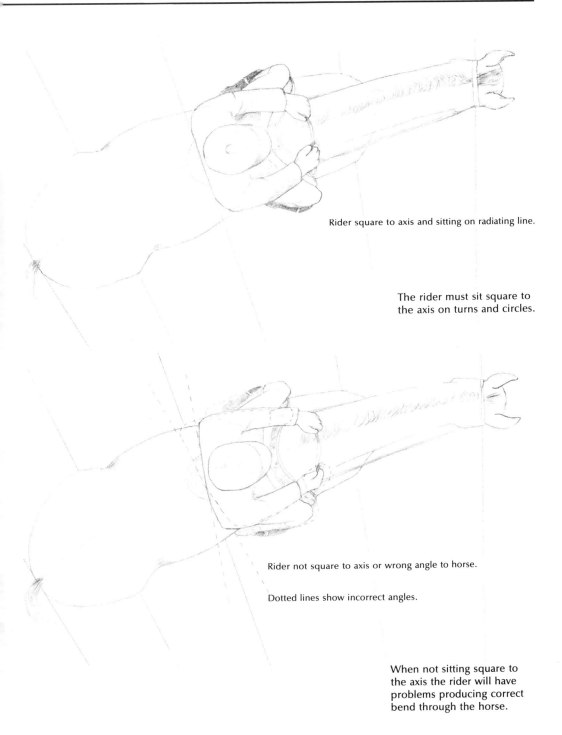

Rider square to axis and sitting on radiating line.

The rider must sit square to
the axis on turns and circles.

Rider not square to axis or wrong angle to horse.

Dotted lines show incorrect angles.

When not sitting square to
the axis the rider will have
problems producing correct
bend through the horse.

The aids given to the horse to explain what is required have been made in a similar manner for hundreds of years the world over. It is important for the trainer to remember that the horse he is dealing with might have no previous experience of their feel, or understand their message, and it is the job of the trainer to explain his meaning clearly to the young or un educated horse. For this reason, they must be given in a positive, straightforward manner. When these aids are applied by the hands, legs, seat etc., they must be made in a way that can be repeated in the same manner over and over again whenever the horse is required to repeat the same actions. Therefore, the simpler the application, the more straightforward the understanding.

When an aid is made more complicated, it is often difficult for the horse to understand its meaning, and equally difficult for the trainer to remember each facet and feel required before the horse will respond and perform. It is therefore better to keep aids simple and uncomplicated, and to reward and praise when the response is carried out correctly. In this way, the horse quickly learns to please, whereas if an unpleasant feel is experienced on such occasions, he would be reluctant to try again.

The trainer has two forms of communication at his disposal – sound and hearing, and feel and touch. Either of these can be supported by a third.

The first of these – communication through sound/hearing, with the horse relating to the sound he hears, not the word used. The second and most used – that of feel/touch applied by the contact of hands, legs and seat to the horse. Both of these can be reinforced by the third form, artificial aids, used to back up the natural aids, but these should not be used as a means of taking short cuts.

Horses are individuals and will respond to the aids in different ways. Where one will respond to the lightest touch another will require great strength. In the early stages of training, for an aid to be explicit, it is sometimes necessary to apply it in a firm, even strong manner. However, each time the aid is repeated, it should be first applied in a lighter manner to try and get the same response from the horse to the lighter feel.

The aids of sound and feel can be used in the following ways:

1. Driving Aids – legs, voice, seat. These aids are energy producing.
2. Restraining Aids – hands, voice, seat. These are aids of control.
3. Supporting Aids – legs, hands, seat. These can be used to assist the driving and restraining aids.

These aids can be supported by artificial aids such as whips, spurs etc.

VOICE AIDS

During the entire training, correct use of the voice can assist the other aids. The first responses to the trainer are usually to the voice aid, even before the horse is ridden, so if given in a correct manner, they can assist throughout the training. It is the tone of voice that is more important than the word used. When the voice command is given, it must be repeated in the same way each time used, until the horse understands its meaning.

LEG AIDS

Because of the position of the rider's legs on the horse when sitting astride, these are the most used of the aids. They should rest, in contact with the horse's side, throughout as much of their length as possible. By increasing and decreasing pressure on the horse's sides, they can gradually teach the horse to travel forward, sideways and backwards when placed in different positions.

Driving Leg To create forward movement, both legs should give firm nudging actions to the sides of the horse in the region of the girth. With an increase of pressure, and sometimes activity, greater energy can be produced. This can either increase length of stride, change the pace, or increase speed or tempo, depending on the supportive action given by the other aids. If one leg is placed behind the girth and used in an active way, its effect will be to drive the quarters to the opposite direction, away from the applied leg.

Rider showing the leg
position 'on the girth'.

Rider showing the leg
position 'behind the girth'.

Supporting Leg This leg can be used to assist the driving leg especially through corners and on circles. If the horse has a tendency to lean on these occasions, he can be supported with a very firm inside leg, which can, at the same time, drive him forward. It can also help direct and support from the outside position by being applied behind the girth in a passive manner to stop the drift of the quarters to the outside.

HAND AIDS

Once energy has been produced by the legs, then it can be controlled by the hands through their action on the reins to the bit.

The amount of control will be determined by the length and the strength put on that rein, and the amount of back-up received from the seat and leg aids. The action of the hand on the short rein is to collect the horse and improve the head and neck carriage. The action of the hand on the long rein is to extend the horse and stretch and relax the muscles, especially along the top of the neck and along his back. Both these actions require that the horse be fully under control, and without this control it is not possible to proceed with training.

Restraining Hand The contact on the rein given by the restraining hand can vary greatly, from the lightest feel given with the fingers, to a much stronger feel given with the action of the arm and hand. The job of the restraining hand is to control energy in conjunction with the action of legs and seat, but not to oppose or prevent it. The uses of the restraining hand are:

1. To ask the horse to relax and flex in poll and jaw.
2. To balance and sustain tempo within a pace.
3. To reduce tempo or make a downward transition.
4. To halt.
5. To rein back.

The restraining action on the rein, however light, can only be applied after the driving aids have produced energy. The hand takes short, firm feels on the rein, to gain the control required. These feels are then followed by a yielding hand. If a sustained restraining action is used, it will result in the horse pulling back on the rider, creating a strong and uncooperative partner. Even when the restraining aid is used to stop the horse, it should still be followed with the yielding action to show the horse he has performed well.

When used to reduce the tempo, or make a downward transition, the restrain on the rein should be counter-balanced by the driving aids, supported by balance and posture in the saddle.

Yielding Hand This is used to show the horse reward for the way he has responded to an aid of control or direction. Its most common use is to follow the restraining aid. When the pressure on the rein is increased, and the horse responds correctly, the rein must then be relaxed or given to create a softer feel on the mouth. This relaxing of the contact can vary from a lightening of the fingers to a complete loosing of the rein, but in each instance it is to show reward. The giving action will help the horse relax and produce lengthening through the neck, thus allowing forward movement.

Supporting Hand This is usually the outside rein used in conjunction with the supporting inside leg. It should not pull backwards, but by a constant steady contact can help prevent the horse falling onto the inside shoulder. Its action can be increased by being taken slightly away from the neck towards the outside, so helping create a more upright horse.

Some horses require a lighter outside hand to allow inside bend and forward movement. In this case the inside hand should take the supportive role. This is achieved by the inside hand taking a steady inside rein towards the neck when travelling through turns and circles. This rein must not pull backwards, and at no time should it cross over the centre line of the neck/wither, to the opposite side, as it then becomes an indirect rein aid which should be totally discouraged.

DIRECTING REIN

This is important to enable the trainer to manoeuvre the horse through turns and circles. Its application can be achieved by very light squeezing to the inside rein in an on-and-off manner, to flex, bend and direct the horse to the turn, or secondly it can be applied by moving the rein to the inside away from the neck to direct the horse without any backward feel on the rein. The second method of opening the rein is the best and most popular, because it leads the horse to the direction required, rather than pulling him.

WEIGHT AND SEAT AIDS

These are produced by sitting in a correct, balanced position, and can influence the movement of the horse in the following ways.

If weight is distributed equally to both seat bones, and the rider pushes down and forward with the pelvis, the effect will be to drive the horse forward. By adopting a feeling of sitting taller in the saddle and bracing the back muscles, assistance will be felt in the collection of the horse, and/or the restraining of forward movement. When riding through turns and circles, more weight should be carried on the inside seat bone, together with a stretched inside leg. This can help the novice's balance and can be developed to act as an aid with the advanced horse.

When using this weight aid, the trainer must be careful not to create one of the biggest faults of any rider – that of collapsing in the waist/hip. It is recognized by the dropping of the shoulder and a slight upward grip of the leg on that side. The effect of this will be to drive the horse to the opposite direction of the collapse so, when this happens on a turn or circle and the collapse is to the inside, the horse can be driven away from the desired direction.

The torso/body of the rider is the largest part, and by distributing his weight forward or backward he can greatly influence forward movement by assisting drive or restraining it. If held in the vertical with a braced back he will aid collection. If held in the vertical with a supple back he will assist and help maintain forward movement. If the rider adopts a body posture too much behind the vertical, he may discourage forward energy, especially with the novice horse, and this will result in the rider riding behind the movement. When constantly carried in front of the vertical, he can cause weakness and lack of control. However, if practised in a balanced way, it may then be adapted for faster paces and jumping.

The co-ordination of the aids and their application is all-important to the result achieved. It is only when they are applied by a rider in a balanced and relaxed position that their full effect can be gained. Should the rider sit in a tense and apprehensive manner, these feels will be transmitted to the horse causing lack of confidence and nervousness.

All aids should be transmitted in a clear and uncomplicated way, so that the horse has no doubt of what is being asked of him, and thus is able to respond correctly.

No abuse or rough handling should ever be applied through the aids, as this can have a long-term adverse effect on a horse, and will only produce a horse who works through fear.

Basic Uses of the Natural Aids	
Seat	Balance
	Control
	Drive
	Collect
Legs	Drive
	Control
	Collect
	Direct
	Bend
Hands	Control
	Direct
	Bend
	Flex
	Collect

Rider adopting a deep position to help engage the horse and produce greater activity.

Rider adopting a light position suitable for a young or novice horse.

One of the trainer's main objectives should be to produce a horse that is a forward, pleasurable ride, showing willing responses to his wishes.

One of the first requirements is to have control of speed and tempo at all paces, and be able to stop without the use of great strength. This control must include turning left and right through circles and turns, with horse and rider remaining in balance. Some of these things the horse will find easy because of natural ability, but other things will only be learned by regular training and practice. The trainer should exercise great control and self-discipline throughout this period, as it is easy to blame the horse for faults which can originate in the rider. It is also important to assess the type of temperament he is dealing with, as it can influence his approach to the work. The majority of horses can be classed into two main groups.

First, the relaxed character who takes an awful lot to upset. He might thus show little regard for the efforts of the trainer, sometimes even showing a stubborn streak. This type must be constantly stimulated and encouraged in his work, and be given great variety to try and enthuse him to do the required job.

Second, there is the opposite, the highly sensitive type, showing signs of nervousness, excitement and hyperactivity. Time and patience must be taken to constantly reassure this type of horse, and he must be praised for every effort shown to please.

The trainer must decide early on if his own temperament is right to train and cope with a particular horse – in some cases a partnership can never be formed because of a clash of temperaments.

MOUNTING

During the early stages of training, the horse should have been taught to stand still whilst being mounted. However, this is sometimes neglected, and the result is a fidgety horse, who is reluctant to stand and difficult to mount.

Time and thought must be given in these cases to decide what might be causing the problem. One reason can be that the horse has been prodded in the ribs by the rider's toe, and hence expects the same thing to happen every time. If this should be the cause, the use of a mounting block will quickly show the horse that mounting is not unpleasant and, if he is rewarded with a titbit at the same time, will soon forget past unpleasantness.

Discomfort can also be felt in the back muscles by the pull and twist on the saddle as the rider pulls himself up. In these cases, the mounting block or an assistant to give a leg-up can again solve the problem. If reluctance to stand is because of excitement or an impetuous temperament, then re-mounting the horse after work and repeating the act three or four times, each time giving a reward, will quite quickly remedy this problem.

THE WALK

To send the horse forward into an active walk, the rider firmly closes his legs to the horse's sides and follows with short nudges in the rhythm of the stride to encourage it forward. If this does not stimulate energy, then the leg aid must be accompanied by voice and whip to urge him forward. The strides should be energetic, and the horse's outline encouraged to stretch forward and down, thus lengthening the top line of the horse and so assisting the development of the muscles in this area.

Should the horse initially show freshness, excitement, or in any way lack control, then the reins must be kept shorter until control is gained, and only then gradually lengthened.

In early stages of training, no attempt should be made to collect the walk, as this can cause irregular and incorrect step sequences which can have a lasting effect and can be difficult to correct. Turns and circles in the walk should be directed by a opening, leading inside rein, as opposed to a pulling or restraining one, which will only shorten the neck and the strides, thus limiting the movement of the horse.

THE TROT

The control maintained in the walk must now be kept during the transition to trot. The reins should first be taken a little shorter to maintain a light contact with the mouth during the

A horse showing a good outline for the novice. There is good activity of stride with equal length in front and behind.

transition, and the trot asked for by an increase of pressure from the legs. A good active pace is required, and to encourage this the first few strides can be taken sitting, which will give the rider maximum use of the aids to stimulate energy.

As much work is likely to be carried out on circles and turns, the trainer must ride on the correct diagonal. This means the rider should sit as the inside hind leg/outside foreleg diagonal comes to the ground, and apply the leg aid at the same time, thus stimulating activity.

A working trot must be encouraged at a good regular tempo, with plenty of energy. On circles to both left and right, a slight bend should also be encouraged throughout the length of the horse to the direction he is travelling, but must not affect the working tempo of the pace. On a circle, the outside rein should regulate and control the horse, and increased drive with the inside leg will help push the horse into the bend and

keep him forward. The inside rein, as in the walk, will direct and lead the head and neck to the desired bend. When the bend is achieved by a push from inside leg into outside rein, it should not be opposed by any backward feel on the inside rein. In fact, intermittent yielding to the inside rein will show the horse a softness to the inside to which he will readily respond and give.

A horse in a long low outline, light on the hand and with a good engagement of stride.

As control to left and right with correct bend is more readily achieved, the horse can be worked through more frequent turns, serpentines and changes of direction, both improving his balance and suppleness. During these exercises, regular transitions should be made to walk and halt to test the responses to the aids. Only if the aids are applied with the same feel and order on each occasion can the horse learn their meaning and will then respond easily.

In the trot, the driving aids should push the horse forward to

A horse on the forehand and heavy on the hand. He shows very little engagement behind or in front.

the contact from the hand. This contact must be a light and comfortable feel, never one that offers strength and lean, as the horse will take support from such a contact, becoming strong and heavy, and putting too much weight on the forehand.

If a horse already has these tendencies, then every effort must be made to correct them early on. Applying short restraining actions on the reins in a regular manner of give and take should liven the contact with the mouth. This, coupled with frequent changes of direction and transitions through the paces to halt, and up again, will help to remedy this uncomfortable problem.

The maintenance of a long, rounded outline is very important, and when the rider is taking the reins shorter for control, they should not be over-shortened, as this will also have a tendency to shorten the neck to such an extent that it will not be easy for the horse to round these muscles and give bend and flexion.

By maintaining the longer neck shape and learning to relax the lower jaw to the feel taken with the hand, the horse will learn to arch the neck, so stretching the muscles over the top of neck and the back (the top line). By this development, a correct rounded outline can be achieved.

No attempt should be made to artificially raise or arch the neck into a more advanced shape, as this only produces resistance to the bit, and teaches the horse to fight the

The head positions of the novice from the raised position on the bit, to the fully extended head and neck on a loose rein.

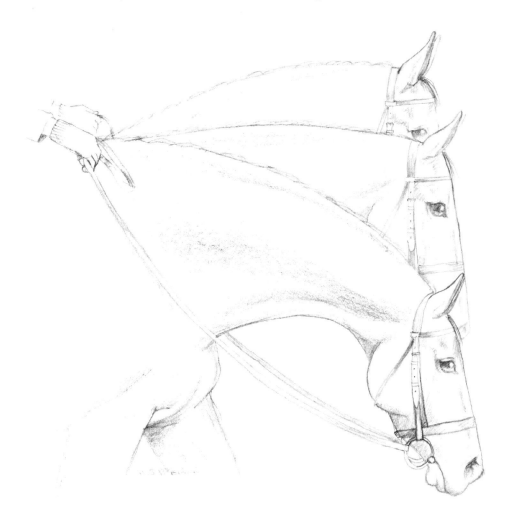

requests of the trainer, producing a hollow outline with fixed or tight back muscles.

Provided the horse is enthusiastic and willing to please, then time and patience should be shown in establishing the roundness and bend throughout this work, and by regular repetition, he will become obedient to the aids. Once sufficient control and obedience have been achieved, then it is time to proceed into canter.

THE CANTER

It is generally thought that a horse with a good walk will have a good canter, and this is often proved correct. A balanced canter is as essential to the riding horse as the walk and trot, and with practice, this can soon be achieved.

Some lack of balance is only to be expected with the novice, but if work has been carried out on the lunge, it should now pay off when performed with the rider.

To assist the balance in the canter, it will be necessary for him to lead with the correct leg. This means that whichever direction he is travelling in, he must lead with the inside foreleg.

Control is of great importance, and it would be foolish to attempt the canter in a wide open space, as should the horse take fright and gallop off, it could undo weeks of work and result in lack of confidence. Ideally, an indoor or outdoor school should be used, otherwise a smallish railed or hedged paddock will help provide the control needed.

Thought must be given to where in the enclosure the canter is best attempted. First, work the horse in the normal routine in walk and trot until he is settled. The canter transition is best asked for when going into a corner, or into the short side of the school (*see* opposite); if asked at this point, he will be more likely to produce the correct lead, because he will want to keep his balance through the corner.

The aids must be very clear and precise to influence the horse and produce the canter. Most horses will give the left lead more readily than the right, and so this is best asked for first. The aids are then applied. Canter left – approach the appropriate corner at a good active trot, on the last few strides go into sitting trot, at the same time maintaining a controlling

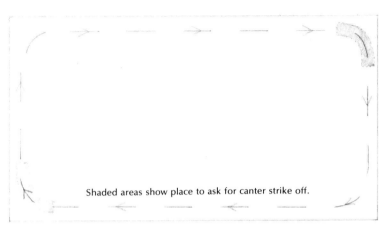

Shaded areas show place to ask for canter strike off.

The shaded areas show where canter strike should be attempted when going right.

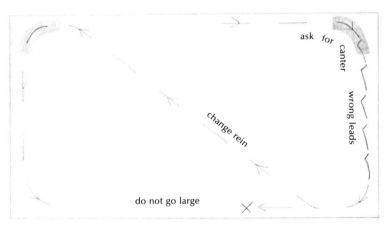

ask for canter

wrong leads

change rein

do not go large

If the wrong canter lead is repeated, change rein to make the canter lead correct.

contact on the reins. Do not lighten the feel on the reins, as this will only allow the horse to go faster in the trot than into the canter. The inside rein (the left) should be taken (as in trot and walk) down and in towards the rider's inside knee. This will direct the head and neck towards the required direction without a backward feel. As this rein aid maintains the head and neck in the required position, the outside leg is drawn back well behind the girth and is applied with a firm nudge, and at the same time the inside leg maintains its normal driving position on the girth. If necessary, the aids can initially be assisted with the voice and whip to produce the required energy.

These aids will normally produce the correct canter lead, but should this not be the case, do not constantly pull him back into trot, as this can discourage further attempts. If the canter has been asked for in the correct corner, but the wrong lead is produced, the trainer who is quickly aware of this situation can take the horse across the diagonal of the school, and by changing the rein, put the horse to the correct canter lead (*see page 53*).

The canter and correct transitions to and from it must become part of the horse's everyday work, as it is only with regular practice that the horse will become balanced. If this canter work is omitted and only practised on rare or special occasions, its infrequency can cause excitement, because of lack of balance and control, and thus hinder his advancement. Once he is confident in this work, it should be included as part of the regular schooling routine, with the transitions through the paces eventually taking an even greater part.

The obedience of the horse in the three basic paces and his ability to perform them correctly is only the start of the work that must eventually be covered. Once these paces can be obtained and sustained with a degree of regularity and balance the rider must then start to link them together so that it is possible to travel through the paces with fluency and ease of movement. Travelling from one pace to another is called a 'transition' and for the novice rider and horse these are generally progressive i.e. from walk, through a few steps into trot, and then into canter. As training progresses they should become more direct i.e. from walk direct into canter. It is therefore important and necessary to practice and improve these transitions in order to enhance the basic paces.

TRANSITIONS

Upward transitions are usually performed with ease, giving few problems, provided a steady rein contact is maintained whilst the leg aids stimulate activity. Should the rein contact be abandoned at this time, the transition will lack control, and the horse will please himself as to how he performs the transition, if at all.

During transitions, the horse should remain in a rounded outline, and if he has a habit of raising the head and neck it will cause a hollow outline. Then, thought should be given as to where the transition is performed, as this can assist the trainer in getting the right responses. If this problem persists, then the transition should be made going into a corner or onto a small circle, using the direct opening rein with a sideways feel, to reinforce the leading of the head down and towards the circle. Resistance can also be caused if the rider tends to over-shorten the reins with a novice horse, thus not giving him sufficient rein to allow him to lower the head and neck. This problem is then made worse, if the rider applies pull to the shortened rein, discouraging forward movement and causing the horse to toss and throw his head in pure frustration at the restriction caused. If it is necessary to shorten the reins, always think 'shorter and lighter'. A lot of small resistances start with little importance, but if allowed to go uncorrected, develop into bad habits, which can label the horse as an uncontrollable ride, simply because the trainer lacks understanding, and does not make corrections early on. Such a horse will not change his habits until he receives corrective training.

Downward transitions require even greater skill from the trainer for correct execution. The rider's legs must be kept in contact with the horse's sides during this time, as they can encourage forward movement as the pace is changed. However, they should not be over-used, as a youngster or novice could be confused and create greater energy than the rider is able to control. The rider's balance must be maintained to assist the horse in keeping his balance through these transitions. Distributing the body weight a little backwards and bracing the back muscles can be of great help when reducing the paces. At first, the transitions should all be progressive; it is only with the mature horse that they become direct. The final control for the downward transitions is the use of the hands,

Well-performed Transition

A well-performed transition is one not requiring strength or force from the rider. It should be performed with ease and not interrupt the smooth flow of energy.

Poor Transition

A poor transition is one that is harsh and abrupt in its application, causing the horse to evade its action with strong resistance.

which assist the legs and body in making the reduction of pace by increasing the rein pressure in an 'on' and 'off' action until the horse responds. If assisted by the voice, the response is quite quickly given, and with a slight lightening of the contact the horse is rewarded. Always avoid the direct, long pull on the reins, as this will create a 'tug-of-war' situation. As the aids are more easily understood, the use of the voice can be lessened and obedience to the aids improved.

When work can be carried out through all three paces in a balanced and obedient manner, then it is time to regulate and influence the tempo of the paces, so starting to improve the rhythm. A greater variety of work can be introduced to add more interest, and a start made as developing the outline and carriage of the horse.

STRAIGHTNESS

A trainer must also become aware of how straight his horse is from head to tail, making sure that the quarters are travelling in the same track as the forehand. We may observe that the horse is straight when he is at liberty, but once he is carrying weight his balance can be upset, and he can quickly develop a tendency to push the quarters left or right, creating movement on two tracks instead of one.

This problem is always corrected by moving the forehand back in front of the quarters, but not by trying to move the quarters either left or right with the leg aids. This could start the horse swaying the quarters to left and right, a problem difficult to correct and control. To move the forehand to one side, the aids must be kept simple. First, treat the forehand as an entire unit, rather than a number of pieces (head, neck, left and right shoulders) as this causes the rider to think of too complicated an aid. To move the forehand to the left, the rider must move the left rein a little to the left, away from the side of the neck, without increasing or decreasing its strength. To support this action, the right rein is taken to the neck, but should not cross over to the left. Increase the support and drive with the inside leg (right) on the girth, and, if necessary, assist the leg aid by placing the whip against the inside shoulder. Do not over-correct, or the horse will escape through the outside shoulder, but remember that when cor-

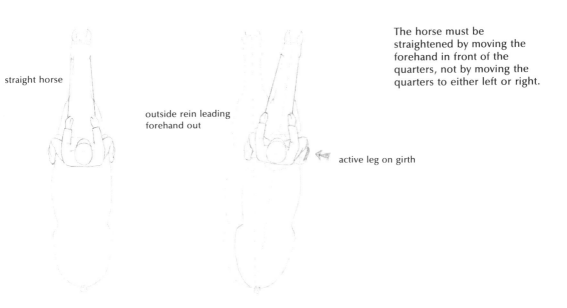

straight horse

outside rein leading
forehand out

The horse must be
straightened by moving the
forehand in front of the
quarters, not by moving the
quarters to either left or right.

active leg on girth

rected, it can re-occur anytime. Forward riding of the horse will also assist the straightening provided he is not taken into too short an outline.

When on a circle, if the horse has a tendency to fall in on the circle, preventing true bend to that direction, it should be rectified in a similar manner.

When changing direction, the novice should change the bend throughout his length each time, and look to the new direction. If the change is made on a long diagonal line, then the horse should be taken through the straight before the bend is changed.

On the straight line, the horse must keep an even contact on both reins, and the rider sit equally astride. When on turns or circles, the rider should try to keep the inside leg stretched in as long a position as possible to assist balance.

In canter, with each change of rein or direction, the novice should return to trot, re-establish his balance, and then be given direction to the new rein, and again be asked to canter with the new leg.

The horse should always be rewarded for any task correctly performed; this need only be a slight lightening of the contact on the inside rein. By this action you show the horse your approval of his efforts.

TRAINING SESSIONS

Notes for the Rider

1. Have aim and purpose in the lesson.
2. Do not argue with the horse – it will only teach him to argue back.
3. Do not demand more than the horse is capable of giving.
4. Know the capabilities of your horse.
5. Do not provoke a resistance.
6. Base your work on the fitness of the horse.
7. Be enthusiastic and encourage work.
8. Always praise and reward.

However muscularly developed a horse appears, it should not be forgotten that it is unwise to ask too much of, or overwork, a young horse. If the lessons are kept short and regular, with reward, the youngster learns very quickly. Overtaxing him and asking too much may produce problems which the trainer might feel are important to tackle, making a small misdemeanour into a big issue.

Sometimes, the older horse may be physically weak because of bad management or lack of regular exercise, and it is necessary to give such horses time, and not put them under too great a pressure, either physically or mentally, before they are ready. Mental strain can be seen in both young and old horses, and usually appears when they have reached the limit of their physical ability. It is a situation that should be avoided.

If the work programme is over-demanding with a sensitive horse, it will have a tendency to excite him, making him difficult to train and control. With this sort of temperament, extra time must be allowed to absorb a lesson, and if a regular routine and timetable be kept to, familiarity will encourage relaxation. Management and diet can also play an important part, because if a horse becomes too fit and well, it can aggravate an already difficult problem. Allowing such horses to spend part of each day at grass, or lungeing before riding, can also assist the trainer. Patience and perseverance are the only way to train this sort of temperament, but the end result is even more rewarding.

Always ride with an objective in mind, and it is wrong to try to school the horse if the trainer is not feeling well. On such occasions, either hack the horse, lunge him or turn him out.

Before demands are made of the horse, the trainer should give thought to what he is trying to achieve, so that he does not make demands incorrectly, causing confusion for the horse. Whatever these demands, every horse will have limitations, because of his build and conformation. For example, the horse with the short neck must be worked in as long a shape as possible, so as not to increase the problem.

Time must be taken in establishing all points in training, so that they are well learned. Failure to do this at all stages will show itself as a weakness later on, and will require the trainer to cover the same ground again, so hindering progress.

Good length of rein allowing good head and neck carriage for novice.

If reins are too short and hand too restricting the horse's neck will be too short not allowing the head forward and down.

This type of work programme will act as an introduction to the sort of discipline that is required, and the attention to detail necessary at this stage of training. This will produce the concentration and precision that will be required later on to produce a horse of a more advanced level. These requirements should also apply to the trainer, as if he cannot approach his work in this way, he cannot expect it of his mount.

(*Above*) A good length of rein to allow a natural head and neck carriage with the novice. (*Below*) If the reins are kept too short, they will restrict the horse's neck and prevent him from adopting natural carriage.

Movement and paces can be influenced by the horse's conformation; this can sometimes show an extravagant or limited stride in some or all of the paces. In the young horse, extravagance or lack of it is usually inherent. However, with the older horse, the quality of movement can have been influenced by earlier training, which may have either improved or restricted his natural movement ability.

If possible, the movement should be observed in its natural state, unrestricted by the weight of the rider. This can be seen either loose in an indoor or outdoor school or on the lunge, when all three paces can be watched.

THE WALK

A horse showing a good active length in a long rein walk.

The following should be seen in a good walk: length of stride, where plenty of overtracking should be seen, and extended head and neck to assist the energetic swing of the stride. Care

must be taken throughout training not to restrict or over-shorten the walk strides, as this can destroy the correct step sequence.

THE TROT

In a working trot, the hind legs should step under the horse to the extent that the hind foot treads into the footprint left by the fore foot. A clear diagonal should be seen, with equal length of stride taken with back and front legs.

A tremendous variation will be seen in the extravagance of this pace, and when a horse shows this extravagance it is very useful when the lengthened strides are required. However, when the horse has this long stride, it can sometimes cause problems when shorter, collected work is desired. If the steps have good energy, rhythm and tempo, then both lengthening and collection will be much easier.

A horse showing a good active trot in a pleasant outline for the novice.

THE CANTER

A very important pace, especially in the training of the dressage and jumping horse. It should show a good swinging action through the body, engaging the hind legs well underneath, and each stride must cover one whole length of his body when in a working tempo. Later in training, it should be possible to collect the pace into a shorter, rounder stride, for more advanced work in both dressage and precision jumping.

If the horse has three good paces, the trainer is fortunate, and his job made easier. However, if the horse has a failing in one or more of his paces, it is up to the trainer to carry out the sort of work which might improve them.

When first ridden, the young horse might lose some of the extravagance seen when moving at liberty. However, if the schooling progresses correctly, he will quickly recover this.

For a poor walk, unrestricted rein length must be given to encourage the lowering and stretching of the neck. A slow tempo should be encouraged to assist in gaining length, because if it is too quick, the walk will quite often be short. If this problem arises, the walk must only be shortened when absolutely necessary, for instance when making upward and downward transitions, or to keep control. Prolonged periods in collection will only restrict and further shorten the strides.

To improve the trot, the trainer must be very aware of rhythm in this two-time pace. If it is kept slow, and the outline kept rounded and long, then extra length of stride can be encouraged. Over-short reins and a fast tempo will only have the effect of shortening and quickening the strides. If the length of the stride made with the front legs is longer than that made with the back legs, then a slight restraining with the hand (to keep a slow tempo) and firm driving aids with the legs (to encourage the hind legs to step under) should make back and front strides more equal.

Two main faults can usually be seen in the canter. The first is the over-shortened horse, where the canter becomes four-time beat. Energetic riding to stimulate the horse and encourage forward movement should re-establish the true canter rhythm and eradicate this problem. The second is the 'heavy on the forehand' type – leaning on the hand and not engaging the back legs. Frequent turns around the quarters and strike-

A horse showing a good engagement of the hind legs in canter and a good length of stride. At this stage the horse is still on the forehand but not heavy on the rein.

offs into canter can help lighten the forehand. During the riding, small circles and transitions can help, and more direct transitions, instead of always thinking they must be progressive, can stimulate the horse to jump into canter, each time lifting and lightening the forehand. Outside activities such as small jumps and riding up and down slopes can also have a similar effect, and help put this problem to rights.

Movement is sometimes restricted through lack of muscle development in certain areas. Correct work and exercise can develop these muscle groups, and subsequently improve the movement. Better movement will be seen when the horse works in a rounded outline, either long or short. This type of work will develop the muscles along the top of the neck, as well as down the back and over the quarters.

Movement can sometimes be lost or impaired if the horse is worked for too long in a shortened shape, or on a short restraining rein which can destroy or restrict the paces.

Most of these problems are rider-related, and it is only if the trainer is aware of them that he is then able to rectify them and prevent faulty action developing further.

To develop a horse to its full potential, the rider must put a lot of daily work into the horse to improve the impulsion, balance and rhythm. Only when this is achieved can he then proceed further in the training.

A horse lacking engagement of the hind legs, although the head and neck show a reasonable position.

The meaning of impulsion is to drive forward, and when applied to a horse it will produce forward movement with energy. However, if it is produced lacking balance and rhythm, the horse will quickly become heavy on the forehand, often out of control, and the trainer must be aware of these problems from the start.

Impulsion is produced by the driving aids of legs and seat/weight; it should not be confused with speed. On the contrary, sometimes greater impulsion can be produced when the horse is engaged at a slower tempo. Should the rider not control this forward energy sufficiently, by letting him run on faster, all the energy produced from the hindquarters is then allowed to escape out of the front. By controlling and regulating this energy with the use of hands, reins and body posture, the rider can develop a more springy, elevated stride. With this development, more weight is taken on the hind quarters, and

If this horse were more engaged behind it would create a better length of neck.

ess on the forehand, thus producing more lightness in the hand. Shifting weight from the forehand to the quarters will have a strong influence on balance, and help to develop the type of outline required to enable the horse to go in self carriage. This lightness of the forehand should be combined with an increased stepping under of the hind legs, and should start to put the horse into a shorter outline, producing the start of collection. This will also influence the balance from left to right, enabling the horse to stay more upright, not only on the straight but also through turns and circles.

Throughout this, rhythm plays a very important role. As the dancer must have a good sense of rhythm, so must the rider, because when schooling he must be the guiding influence.

By slowing down or speeding up the application of the driving aids, it is possible to develop or destroy the natural rhythm of the horse. When influencing movement in this way, the rider must be very aware of the natural tempo produced, and must then decide if it needs pacifying or stimulating to improve it.

By developing the rider's ability to apply the driving aids, movement of the horse should be improved and it should flow in a more regular way, showing ease and suppleness and thus making a more pleasant ride.

Some horses are able to produce very good rhythm on their own, and the rider must be careful not to destroy this. Others may show many variations of speed and the rider must try and keep a regular steady tempo to influence the horse in the same manner.

To perform turns and circles correctly, the horse must be capable of lateral flexion and lateral bend. Flexion should not be confused with bend – they are very different things. When the horse is giving lateral bend, he must also be giving flexion in the same direction.

To give lateral flexion, the horse must relax in his poll, and slightly turn the head in the direction asked, without bending through his neck and body. When this flexion is given in a submissive manner, the trainer will be able to observe the muscles in the crest of the neck rolling over the spine in the direction of the flexion. Initially, this rolling action may cause the horse a little concern when he first experiences this strange sensation; for this reason, it is sometimes best taught from the ground.

Horse and rider showing unity around the left circle, upright and in balance.

Stand facing the horse's head, and take a rein in each hand close to the bit rings. Slightly increase the pressure to one side of the bit to turn the head very slightly, without putting bend in the neck. This is lateral flexion. If the crest of the neck is watched during this action, it will be seen to flip over to the direction of the flexion asked. This same reaction is then asked for by the rider when mounted, and when the horse responds the rein must immediately yield to show him he has done this correctly. Once flexion has been taught, it should be used in conjunction with bend through turns and circles, and when on the straight this flexion must again be given without bend to the direction of travel.

Bend consists of curving the horse throughout his body length to left and right. The amount of curve is dependent on the shape being ridden. It is wrong to create greater bend in the neck than in the body, or to bend greater than the curve of the circle or turn. Sometimes we see the rider snapping the horse just in front of the shoulder when the neck is turned rather like the rudder of a boat, and this is totally incorrect. When taking bend to the direction wanted with a directing or leading inside rein, the amount of bend taken must be regulated by the outside rein.

The horse must learn to submit equally to left and right, and perform turns to each direction without showing stiffness or resistance to one side.

Frequent work and many changes of direction will provide the rider with numerous opportunities to test and improve the horse's ability to bend and turn until it can be performed with

ease. The horse must not resist a bend by popping his quarters to the opposite direction and falling in on his shoulder.

All turns in the arena should be ridden as a quarter of a circle. It would be wrong to expect a greater response from a novice horse. The rider's inside leg used to support and activate the horse will also assist in gaining bend to the desired direction.

When changing direction from one circle to another (figure of eight), the inside hand asks for bend and flexion. To prevent the horse falling to the new direction, the rider's inside leg and outside rein will have a stronger influence to assist balance. These aids are also repeated when riding serpentines, these being only linked-up half circles.

Teaching the horse turns on the forehand and haunches can

A horse drifting away from the right circle through the left shoulder.

A horse showing flexion to the right, asked for from the ground.

A horse showing flexion to the left, asked for from the ground.

give the rider greater control over the front and back of the horse, and they also teach the horse to move away from the individual leg aids.

TURN ON FOREHAND

This teaches the horse to move the quarters away from a sideways driving leg. Halt the horse parallel to the long side of

A horse and rider on a straight line, with the horse straight and the rider sitting equal to left and right.

the arena, but to the inside of the track to allow the horse enough room for the turn. Take a light feel on the outside rein to get flexion in that direction. Move the leg on the same side to behind the girth, and with an active driving action, push the quarters to the opposite direction until a full 180 degree turn is completed, and the horse is facing the direction from which he came. During the turn, he should not be allowed to step backwards and this is prevented by the leg aids sending the horse to the bit.

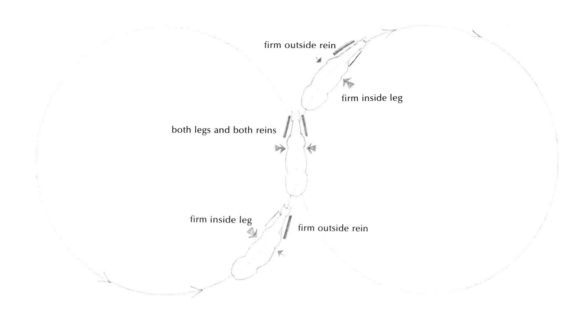

firm outside rein

firm inside leg

both legs and both reins

firm inside leg

firm outside rein

Leg and rein aids for riding from one circle into another.

TURN ON HAUNCHES OR HALF PIROUETTE

This will assist with the collection of the horse and the lightening of the forehand. At novice level, it is performed in walk and the bend and flexion is taken to the inside (the direction to which the forehand will turn). Move this rein sideways away from the neck to lead the forehand to the turn. The rider's weight is increased to the inside seat bone, the inside leg is long and against the girth area to keep the horse forward to the bit. The outside leg is applied behind the girth to prevent the quarters swinging out away from the turn. It can also move forward to be applied in the girth area and initiate the first steps taken by the forelegs to the inside. At this level, it is permissible for the inside hind leg to tread a small circle, rather than become stuck, and pivot on the spot. The outside treads a larger circle around the inside one, but should not be allowed to step back or away from the circle (*see* opposite). Both hind legs keep active, taking short steps. The front legs tread a larger circle around the small one made by the hind legs.

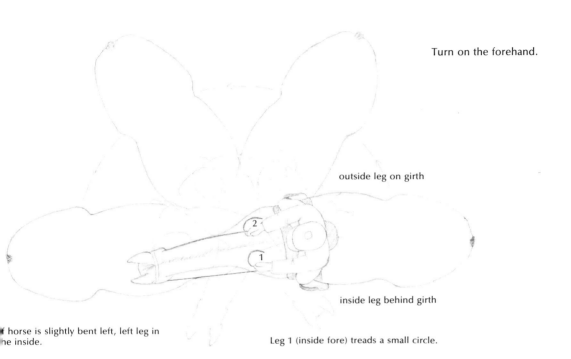

Turn on the forehand.

outside leg on girth

inside leg behind girth

horse is slightly bent left, left leg in
he inside.

Leg 1 (inside fore) treads a small circle.

Turn on the haunches
or half pirouette.

inside leg on girth

outside leg behind girth

Leg 2 (inside hind) must tread a small circle.

Signs of Fitness and Health

1. Bright, alert appearance.
2. Good sheen and texture to coat.
3. Enthusiasm to work.
4. Cool, hard appearance to the legs.
5. Good muscle development.
6. Hard, well-shaped feet.
7. Free, regular movement.
8. Neither over or under weight.

As the training programme progresses, it should develop into an enjoyable experience for both horse and rider.

It is important occasionally to stand back and take stock of the situation to see that things are progressing in the way required. It is necessary for the horse to be respectful of the rider's wishes, and to do this he must be very clear in his mind what he is required to do and how. There must be no grey uncertain areas, everything must be very clear. At the same time, the rider must have respect for his horse, never losing his temper, and always trying to understand and build a polite relationship of trust and reward. Only on these terms can a lasting association be built. If it is built on threat, fear and punishment, the horse will constantly try to evade the rider's aids, and be reluctant to work or please.

Not all training is straightforward, and not all horses co-operative. They should be dealt with by firm handling, and riding with corrections being made when necessary. Most horses will then soon start to do what is asked of them.

In these situations, it is important for a rider to recognize when a battle is won, and then to instantly reward the horse, taking care not to pursue an argument or to 'nag on' about it, only to provoke the same trouble again.

The horse's educational development is also dependent on his fitness and health. If he is not feeling 100 per cent, he is not going to give of his best, and a good trainer must be quick to recognize and deal with any form of ill health. The unschooled or novice horse can quite often suffer from slight muscle stiffness when first asked to perform regular work, and this is a consideration that must be kept in mind when asking for performance.

The horse should always be kept in good health and fitness. However, getting him over-fit and well too soon can also produce problems for his rider. To carry out a reasonable day's work, it is not necessary for him to be leaping out of his skin with freshness.

Over-fitness can sometimes be detrimental to the horse and cause undue strain because of the amount of extra work that has to be given to get rid of the freshness. This can take longer than the schooling session. Mental concentration will also be difficult to maintain in these circumstances, again having an adverse effect on his work.

It is the responsibility of the trainer to keep a check on the

Correct work can help develop the right muscle groups and change the outline of the horse. (*Above*) Shaded areas show the areas that develop with good work. (*Below*) The weak, under-developed horse – lack of muscles make it almost impossible for him to work in a correct outline.

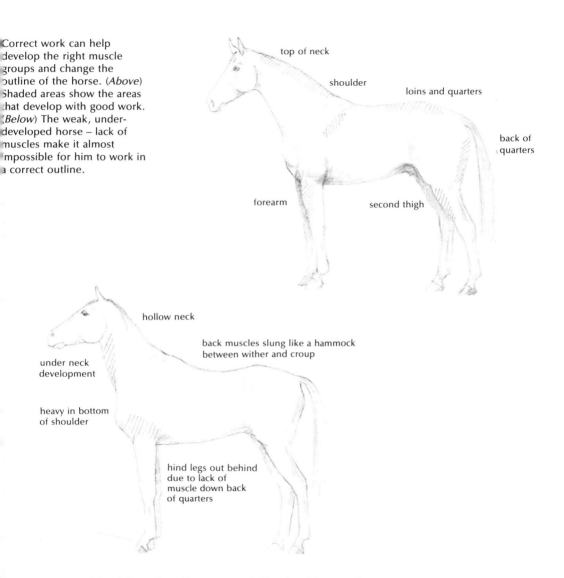

top of neck

shoulder

loins and quarters

back of quarters

forearm

second thigh

hollow neck

back muscles slung like a hammock between wither and croup

under neck development

heavy in bottom of shoulder

hind legs out behind due to lack of muscle down back of quarters

horse's general health and welfare, especially checking on leg conditions. These checks should ensure that the work is not causing strain or problems in this area, but if recognized early, a major problem can quite often be overcome. So, stand back occasionally, take a good look at both the horse and the situation to see that progress is being made. It is quite easy to get so involved with one thing that it is possible to overlook a point of major importance.

A few of the most common problems relate to everyday life, and involve the basic requirement of obedience. Although it may not be necessary, always have an assistant around who can give a hand if need be, as it is better to be safe than sorry. The horse is a very large and powerful animal, and any sort of argument should not be taken lightly. At times, a rider must be quite bold in giving a quick reprimand to correct a problem, and he will need to be secure and balanced in position.

However diligently and correctly the training is carried out, it is seldom trouble-free. Problems are not always rider-related, and can be bad habits learned or inherited from other horses, or stimulated by environment or circumstances. However, they do become the problem of the rider, and it is often his job to try and put them right.

NAPPING AND SHYING

One of the most common riding problems is that a horse refuses to go forward to the leg aids, and tries to 'nap'. This resistance sometimes happens when trying to leave the stable environment, or when being asked to leave other horses. Being a herd animal, this tendency may be an inherent one, and may be because the horse lacks confidence to proceed on his own. However, it is the job of trainers and riders to try and assume the position of leader of that herd, and instil confidence where it is lacking.

When dealing with a young horse, much can depend on the attitude of the trainer. He must always be bold in his approach, encouraging the horse to respond in a similar way. With such horses, never get lulled into a daily routine, where the horse knows where he is going and when things will happen. This only gives him time to plan and prepare his disobedience. The rider who adopts a bold attitude with a young horse, taking him off on his own and doing a variety of work will seldom encounter this type of problem. More often, it is encountered with the horse that has been cossetted and protected, kept in a secure environment, usually in the company of other horses, which he then finds increasingly difficult to leave. These habits, once formed, are very difficult to break, and so it is better to try and avoid them altogether with a bolder approach from the start.

When these problems do exist in an older horse, they can prove more difficult to correct. It is because of uncorrected repetition that the horse has found a weakness in his rider. Whereas the problem might have been caused initially because of lack of confidence, even fear, this can totally turn about and be the horse's way of showing his dominance over the rider.

In these cases, when all efforts at coaxing and tempting have been tried, the rider may be forced to have a confrontation

with the horse, and administer sharp, quick punishment with the whip to prove his dominance. Always be quick to sense the horse's submission, and immediately praise and reward him when he responds favourably. Be careful to deal with this type of problem in safe surroundings and on safe going. It would be unwise to tackle this on a slippery road surface near a ditch or barbed wire fence, because if control is lost in this situation it can cause serious damage to either horse or rider.

Occasionally, this type of problem can be caused by the horse being asked to perform a job which he is not happy doing e.g. being a dressage horse if he would rather go cross country. The remedy in this sort of situation is fairly easy to rectify by ensuring more variety in his work, or even thinking of letting him go into a different career.

Care must be taken if you are riding an older horse who has 'nappy' tendencies with a youngster, as it can be catching once observed, and before you know it, he will try it himself.

The shying horse can also be a problem, and it can be even

When a horse 'naps' he will stop and often turn away from the required direction. In this evasion he will normally turn away to the left.

quite dangerous if on the roads. The habit may be caused by a number of reasons, such as nervousness, freshness, habit, or just trying to play up and test the rider. Whatever the cause, the rider must try to gain control and ensure prevention.

When riding such horses, the rider must be constantly attentive to anything that might cause him to be startled. Riding along on a loose rein, chatting to a friend and not concentrating on the job is asking for trouble. One of the most common mistakes is to turn him to face the frightening object. Once his total attention is taken in this way, he will not be capable of listening to the rider's aids, and will quite often spin away. To counter this reaction, the head and neck must be bent away from the offending object, and the leg aids increased to drive the horse past in a leg yield position (*see* opposite).

If, at the beginning of exercise, this problem is caused by freshness, the rider must sit deep and firm to drive the horse forward at a good energetic pace, and thus gain control of this excess energy. Firm riding is the only way to produce the control needed in these situations. As he matures, these habits should diminish, but take care, as they can suddenly reappear, taking the rider totally by surprise.

LACK OF CONTROL

This is a very unpleasant situation to cope with and, in the extreme, can result in a run-away situation. First, check the rider; by sitting and riding in an unbalanced position, the rider can produce problems for the horse, causing him to run out of control. Rough treatment administered through the bit with hard hands can cause great discomfort, and the horse may try to run away from it. The rider should seek tuition to rectify the riding problem first. If a horse lacking control is acquired for training, the first step must be to have the mouth and teeth checked by a vet to ensure that no treatment is necessary there. The horse must then be sympathetically bitted, perhaps with a rubber snaffle or at least a snaffle with a thickish mouthpiece to give him stability and comfort. If he has developed the habit of opening his mouth, then a firmly adjusted flash or drop noseband will help this problem.

A mouth problem can sometimes be caused by the horse not

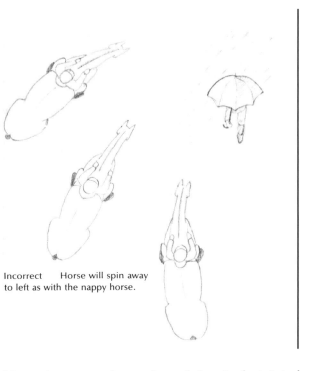

Incorrect   Horse will spin away to left as with the nappy horse.

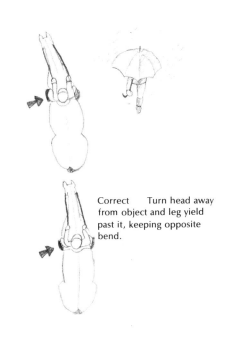

Correct   Turn head away from object and leg yield past it, keeping opposite bend.

(*Left*) The shying horse, and (right) the correct way to approach a frightening object.

liking the nutcracker action of the single jointed snaffle, and when changed to the French link snaffle with a double joint, or the straight or mullen mouth snaffle, the response from him can be totally changed. Sometimes it pays to experiment a little with a different type of snaffle.

All horses with these sorts of problems should be ridden in an environment where maximum control can be maintained, until the rider feels more confident about being able to keep sufficient control to venture further afield. At all times, a kind and sympathetic approach must be used, which will require great patience, but full control will not be achieved until the horse is totally confident.

Incorrect riding may mean that the horse develops a very hollow outline and a very strong underneck. These types can be difficult to re-school, especially older horses that may have continued in this manner for some years. It might prove advantageous in such cases to use a correctly adjusted running martingale, to assist the rider in his early attempts to correct this difficult problem.

Control problems with the younger horse may be easily avoided if he receives correct riding and training from the start.

A bad riding surface showing irregular and rough terrain.

The important points related to the young or novice horse are as follows:

Surfaces Artificial surfaces are obviously more consistent all the year round, but the horse must become accustomed to all types of surfaces and terrain to make a good all-rounder.

Weather There is greater comfort for horse and rider indoors, but the horse cannot spend all his life indoors, and through being in the elements he will learn to cope with all changes of climate – wind, rain, snow, sun, irritation by flies, and slippery and hard underfoot conditions. The horse must learn to concentrate in any conditions, and this will only be learned by being exposed to these elements.

Concentration This is more easily learned indoors, but usually has to be re-learned when the horse is taken outside. By combining inside and outside, lessons learned inside can then be practised outside and progress made.

Temperament The sensitive or excitable horse is probably better trained indoors, as more concentration is possible. However, to compete outside, the horse must also be schooled outside. Again, a combination of both will probably be beneficial.

A well-maintained riding surface, giving constant, ideal ground conditions.

Coming and going of other horses If a young horse worries about the arrival or departure of other horses, the lesson is best learned inside, as control is more easily maintained with four walls to help. Once control is established, it can then be attempted outside.

Obviously, it is beneficial to have both indoor and outdoor facilities, and it can certainly be an advantage to have an indoor arena. However, the same lessons can be achieved outside, though a little more time will probably be necessary to achieve the same result, but once learned this way, they will be more thoroughly learned.

Good Basic Training can prepare the horse for a number of riding disciplines including:

Hunting
Show Jumping
Eventing
Dressage
Hacking
Endurance

They all require:
Obedience
Balance
Athletic ability
Fitness

He will be required to:
Walk
Trot
Canter
Gallop
Jump

depending on his involvement with each sport.

Basic training must cover as much ground as possible to develop the horse into an all-round athlete capable of a variety of work. It should include work on the flat, pole work, gymnastic jumping, and general riding over a variety of terrain.

This work can be begun in conjunction with the flat work, and the youngster can start as soon as his physique is developed, and the rider has sufficient control over direction in the three basic paces.

Simple pole work can be started in walk, placing them at random around the schooling area, so they can be included in the routine work programme. Once the horse accepts their inclusion calmly, the same work can be done in trot. This will improve rhythm and regulate the length of stride if the tempo is kept calm and regular. From single poles, groups can be introduced, varying from two or three up to five or six at a time; as well as straight lines, they can be placed around the perimeter of a large circle where each pole must radiate from the centre point. This allows the trainer to use a longer or shorter stride for the horse, by trotting a larger or smaller circle. The distance between poles will depend on the horse's stride, and must be adjusted to suit. This can vary between 4ft (1.2m) and 4ft 6in (1.4m) between each pole. The rider must try to maintain the rounded outline in the horse, getting him to use the muscles along the top line, and assist him by using the rising trot at a good rhythmical tempo.

Rider and horse should stay relaxed and calm, as tension and tightness can destroy the benefit of this work by causing irregular strides and restricted movement, often combined with lack of control when approaching and going over the poles. Ideally, the outline and manner of going should stay the same as on the flat, allowing freedom of movement and showing enjoyment of work. If he should show excitement, tending to rush at the poles, then the walk should be resumed with the use of the voice to calm him, and a variety of approaches be made to avoid anticipation. This can sometimes be improved by shorter approaches from turns and circles. Only resume the work in trot once relaxation is achieved in walk. However, should the problem persist, then a brief period being lunged over the poles might help, and establish the confidence and relaxation that will be required when ridden. Once this work is established in a correct manner, then he can progress to jumping small fences.

JUMPING ON THE LUNGE AND LOOSE

It might be beneficial to lunge or loose school over small jumps before attempting this mounted. This can allow total freedom over a fence, and give the horse time to think for himself.

LUNGE JUMPING

This should not be overdone, and the trainer should not become over ambitious too soon, as it can destroy confidence.

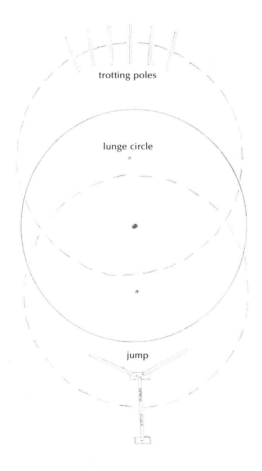

trotting poles

lunge circle

jump

From the basic lunge circle the horse can be taken to one side to include trot poles and the other side to include a small jump.

Types of Fences and Their Uses

Spreads – will stretch the horse and lengthen the stride.
Uprights – will shorten the strides and teach the horse to jump off its hocks.
Grids and Lanes – will improve fluency and gymnastic ability.
Cross County – will teach the horse to think and cope with natural fences and uneven terrain.

Jumping the young or novice horse over large fences on the lunge can cause much stress and strain, because of the effort of the jump and the tightness of the circle.

Lunge first in the normal manner in tack with side-reins attached. Place a pole on the perimeter of the circle, and get the horse used to its inclusion. When settled, change it for a small fence. Once this stage is reached, remove the side-reins to allow the horse maximum freedom of movement of the head, neck and back whilst jumping the fence.

The fence should be positioned in such a way that it can be included or bypassed by the horse, as it will not be jumped on each rotation of the lunge. A slanting pole must be placed against the wing of the fence, so the lunge line slides up and over it without getting snagged on the fence and frightening the horse.

Only include the fence when the horse is settled and concentrating on his job. If seeing the fence causes excitement and speed, it should be bypassed, and only included again when the horse has settled. The lunger must be prepared to move with the horse on a parallel line, so he can present him straight to the jump and maintain control on landing.

Beware of testing the horse over high fences on the lunge, as this can destroy confidence rather than improve it. It places tremendous strain on the legs and tendons, and so quite often slows progress rather than advances it.

LOOSE JUMPING

If the right facilities are available, loose jumping is probably better than lungeing, as the horse has total freedom, thinks for himself, and can learn relative distances between fences without the hindrance of the rider.

Lane construction is easy in the indoor or outdoor school, with the use of poles and wings. This is not as easy in a field, and good fencing is needed to confine the horse to the lane. However, it can be well worth the effort of building, proving extremely beneficial with both novice and older horses. The temporary lane can be constructed in an arena. It should be approximately 10ft (3m) to 12ft (3.5m) wide down the long side; do not include the jumps until the horse is accustomed to going down the lane.

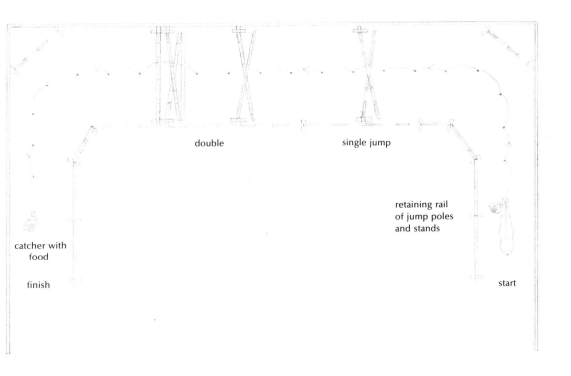

double   single jump

retaining rail
of jump poles
and stands

catcher with
food

finish   start

The horse need only wear a headcollar and protective boots, and is led to the lane by one handler, who encourages him down the lane. The second handler collects him at the other end and rewards him.

Small fences are then included at relative distances, to test the horse's mental and physical ability by letting him sort out his own problems and organize himself. A greater variety of fences can be introduced, including uprights, spreads and parallels, but all should be accurately spaced to encourage fluency through the fences. Bounce, one-stride or two-stride combinations can be included and distances should be measured correctly. In the canter, the bounce stride combination should measure approximately 11–12ft (3–3.5m) between obstacles, the one non-jump stride combination is approximately 21–24ft (6.5–7m) between obstacles, and the two non-jump stride combination are 32–34ft (10–10.5m). These canter stride measurements must be adjusted according to the horse's canter stride, some being much shorter striding than

A loose jumping lane built down the long side of an indoor or outdoor arena. This lane includes a single fence and a double, at related distances. Distances must be adjusted to suit long or short striding horse or pony.

others. The objective when starting jumping is not to trick or confuse the horse, but to make his task as enjoyable as possible before proceeding to larger fences.

RIDING FENCES

Once the horse is ridden over fences, the primary objective must be to make the exercise enjoyable, and accustom him to a variety of obstacles both in terms of design and shape, rather than simply trying to jump big fences.

As in flat work, horses will show a variety of styles and attitudes when jumping. The right sort of work will develop a horse's technique, and teach him to round over a fence and perform a correct bascule.

Jumping from the trot can teach the horse to round over a

Riding uphill in the forward position.

fence by placing trot poles in front of a fence, (approximately 10ft (3m) away is average, and the jump approximately 2ft (.75m) high). This type of exercise encourages the horse to elevate the forehand from a slower speed, rather than the faster canter which can sometimes flatten the horse.

With the development of physique and ability, more obstacles can be added to these exercises and they can be made more testing – the true test is being able to ride a small course of fences at approximately 2ft 6in (.75m) to 3ft (1m) high with comparative ease and calmness. It is also necessary to ride the horse across country, both on the flat and over obstacles. To give a pleasurable ride, the horse must be balanced and obedient. He must first learn to cope with uneven terrain, and go up- and downhill first in walk, and then in trot and canter. During jumping and cross country riding it is necessary for the rider to adopt a balanced forward position, giving the horse

Riding downhill in the forward position – not out of control or unbalanced.

Riding downhill in the
balanced upright position.

freedom through his back at all paces, both uphill and down.
For a balanced forward position, the rider should take up a
shorter stirrup, so that the seat can be slightly lightened. He
then inclines the body slightly forward, so that shoulders,
knees and toes form a vertical line. As before, this will slightly
vary with the individual's personal physique and the rider must
be capable of maintaining this position over all types of terrain
and obstacles.

With all types of riding across country, it can sometimes be
helpful to have the assistance of an experienced lead horse
with the novice, to give confidence in unusual circumstances.
It can also be an asset when first introduced to water and small
ditches; these should be in a very simple, uncomplicated form
to avoid problems. All work must be treated as fun, trying to
avoid any frightening experiences that could mar the horse's
confidence in the long term.

The majority of horses 'come alive' in this type of situation,
even the quietest being keen and sometimes over-enthusiastic.
Show patience in these initial stages to encourage this enthusiasm, whilst trying to control and train it, so you are able to

enjoy the pleasure given by the horse whilst a partnership is formed.

A horse and rider, confident and happy, enjoying jumping a course.

Tips for Safe Riding
1. A riding hat should always be worn.
2. Wear suitable footwear.
3. Equipment should be cleaned and checked regularly.
4. Have a basic knowledge of first aid for horse and rider.
5. Observe safety procedures. Display no smoking signs and emergency telephone numbers.
6. Enjoy riding but don't fool around or play practical jokes on horse or rider – it can cause accidents.
7. Once a horse is stabled or confined he is totally reliant on his owner for his daily needs – make sure you are prepared to provide this – every day.

This apprenticeship period for the horse is probably the most important period of his training, if not of his life. If these basics are well-established, they can be of lifelong assistance to the horse, and can always be referred to when problems arise.

Following this initial period of training, it should be possible to decide where the horse's future lies. It might be that the trainer has no ambition to take the horse further, but be quite content to enjoy a well-schooled all-round ride.

For those who are more competitive-minded, it should be decided into which field the horse shows most talent, and whether the rider has the same ambitions. It should be possible to decide if his personality is right for the job, and if he will proceed in a cooperative manner when put under more pressure. Only after assessing these points, can it be decided if the horse is worth a lot of time and effort, to hopefully fulfill his potential and be enjoyed for many years.

The well-schooled horse should provide a pleasurable ride.

However far a trainer takes a horse, it is never a waste of time, and experience will be gained with every horse, each one proving a new and exhilarating experience.

Aids The means by which the rider communicates with the horse.

Artificial Aids Items such as spurs, whips, martingales used to assist the natural aids.

Artificial Surface Riding arenas constructed of materials such as wood chips, sand, plastic to give a consistent surface throughout the year.

Balance The horse is balanced when he can carry himself in an upright manner through turns, circles and movements at all paces, with his weight equally distributed over his forehand and quarters.

Bascule The rounded shape the horse's body makes from head to tail to form an arch over the top of a jump.

Bend The lateral curve produced through the horse from head to tail to enable him to travel correctly through turns and circles.

Bits Bits are placed in the horse's mouth to enable the rider to transmit his wishes to the horse via their feel.

Bounce fence Two jumps separated by a measured distance where the horse will jump, land and jump without a stride in between.

Canter lead When the horse is viewed in canter one foreleg will appear to preceed the other when contact is made with the ground – this is the canter lead.

Carriage The manner in which the horse carries himself, with a high or low head carriage.

Cavesson A piece of equipment worn by the horse on its head to give the trainer control when lungeing and training without having hold of the horse's mouth.

Changing rein Changing the direction to which you are riding.

Collection The shortened outline of the horse producing a shorter arc through the horse, with shorter and more elevated steps.

Combination A line of two or three jumps placed at relative distances where the horse will take one or two strides between each jump.

Conformation The general outline of the horse produced by the make and shape of the body and its extremities.

'D's The small D-shaped attachments on the front of a saddle or roller to which other pieces of equipment can be attached.

Diagonal line A line that can be ridden across the arena from one corner to the other.

Diagonal strides The trot is produced by the horse jumping from one diagonal pair of legs to the other pair – this is termed the 'diagonal' in the trot.

Direct transition When the horse travels from walk into canter or from canter to walk without going through trot.

Engaged When the horse's hindlegs are placed well under the body and so take more weight than the forelegs.

Extended The horse is extended when he lengthens his outline and his stride without quickening and thus covers more ground.

Flatten   The horse is said to flatten over a jump when he does not produce a rounded arc (bascule) through his body.

Flexion   Movement produced in the junction between the head and neck, either from up to down, or from side to side.

Forehand   The front of the horse including head, neck, shoulders and forelegs.

Forward position   The riding position used when schooling the young horse, riding over jumps, or riding the extended canter and gallop.

Fourtime Canter   An incorrect leg sequence in the canter pace producing a fourtime beat instead of a threetime one.

Freshness   The state in which the horse is over exuberant, sometimes caused by underwork or overfeeding.

Hand contact   The feel held by the hands, down the reins to the bit.

Haunches   The back part of the horse including the quarters and hind legs.

Hollow   The horse that carries the head and neck too high with a slack back giving overall impression of looking hollow in the outline.

Leading   The action of walking with the horse rather than riding him.

Lead horse   One used to encourage another by going in front to give confidence.

Loose school   The horse is allowed to go at liberty within a riding arena or school.

Lungeing   Training the horse to make a circle around the lunger to improve his balance.

Lunge line   The line held by the trainer to control the horse whilst being lunged.

Movement   The strides produced by the horse in walk, trot or canter.

Napping   A horse that refuses to proceed when and where he is asked, disobeying the trainer.

Numnah   A thin or thick pad placed between the saddle and the horse to make carrying weight more comfortable.

Outline   The overall shape produced by the horse when in action.

Outside rein   When riding a circle or turn, the outside rein is always the one on the opposite side to the direction of travel.

Overtracking   The gap produced when the hind foot overtreads the print left by the forefoot.

Paces   The horse has four basic paces – walk, trot, canter and gallop.

Pole work   Riding over poles placed on the ground at relative distances.

Progressive transitions   When the horse moves from walk to canter he must progress through the trot.

Quarters   The large muscle mass above the hindlegs over the pelvic area.

Rein stops Small pieces of leather or rubber that attach to the reins near the bit to prevent the rings of the running martingale slipping over the buckles and becoming trapped.

Roller A type of wide belt worn around the body of the horse just behind the forelegs to which other equipment can be attached.

Rhythm The regularity with which a horse places his feet on the ground in all paces.

Self carriage When a horse is able to carry himself in a correct outline with balance, without being held there by a strong contact down the reins.

Shying The action the horse produces to avoid going near something he is frightened of.

Snaffle The simplest and mildest form of bit used for schooling.

Straightness The horse is said to be straight when forehand and quarters follow in the same line with no deviation to left or right.

Strike off The first step into the canter pace.

Surcingle A narrow webbing strap placed over the top of a saddle for added security.

Tempo The speed at which the horse travels in each pace.

Topline The line along the top of the horse starting behind the ears, along the top of the neck, along the back and over the quarters to the tail.

Track The line ridden around the perimeter of the school.

Transitions Riding the horse from one movement or pace to another.

Underneck The muscles on the underside of the neck.

Yielding hand The hand that gives the rein contact towards the horse's mouth.

Association of British Riding Schools
Miss A Lawton
Old Brewery Yard
Penzance
Cornwall   TR18 2SL

British Horse Society
British Equestrian Centre
Stoneleigh
Kenilworth
Warwickshire   CV8 2LR

British Field Sports Association
General J Hopkinson
59 Kennington Road
London   SE1 7PZ

**British Show Hack, Cob and
Riding Horse Association**
Mrs R Smith
Rockwood
Packington Park
Meriden
Warwickshire   CV7 7HF

British Show Jumping Association
British Equestrian Centre
Stoneleigh
Kenilworth
Warwickshire   CV8 2LR

British Warmblood Society
Mrs D Wallin
Moorlands Farm
New Yatt
Witney
Oxfordshire   OX8 6TE

**Hunters Improvement and National
Light Horse Breeding Society**
G W Evans
96 High Street
Edenbridge
Kent   TN8 5AR

National Equine Welfare Committee
c/o Bronsby Home of Rest for Horses
Bransbury
Near Saxilby
Lincolnshire   LN1 2PH

National Foaling Bank
Meretown Stud
Newport
Shropshire   TF10 8BX

National Stud
Newmarket
Suffolk   CB8 0XE

Riding for the Disabled Association
Avenue R
National Agricultural Centre
Stoneleigh
Kenilworth
Warwickshire   CV8 2LY

Royal Agricultural Society of England
A D Callaghan
National Agricultural Centre
Stoneleigh
Kenilworth
Warwickshire   CV8 2LZ

Side Saddle Association
Mrs M James
Highbury House
Welford
Northamptonshire   NW6 7HT

Worshipful Company of Saddlers
The Clerk
Saddlers Hall
Gutter Lane
Cheapside
London   EC2V 6BR

American Farriers Association
4089 Iron Works Pike
Lexington, KY 40511

American Grandprix Association
P.O. Box 495
Wayne, PA 19087

American Horse Council
1700 K St., NW
Suite 300
Washington, DC 20006

American Horse Protection Association
1000 29th St., NW, #T-100
Washington, DC 20007

American Horse Shows Association
220 E. 42nd St.
Suite 409
New York, NY 10017

American Riding Instructor Certification
Program
P.O. Box 4076
Mount Holly, NJ 08060

American Veterinary Medical Association
930 Meacham Rd.
Schaumberg, IL 60196

National 4-H Council
7100 Connecticut Ave.
Chevy Chase, MD 20815

North American Riding For The
Handicapped Association
P.O. Box 33150
Denver, CO 80233

United States Combined Training Association
292 Bridge St.
South Hamilton, MA 01982

United States Dressage Federation
P.O. Box 80668
Lincoln, NE 68501

United States Pony Clubs
893 Matlock St., #110
West Chester, PA 19382

United States Professional Horsemen's
Association
4059 Ironworks Pike
Lexington, KY 40511

United States Equestrian Team
Gladstone, NJ 07934

Crossley, Anthony *Training the Young Horse: The First Two Years*

d'Enrody, Lt Col A L *Give Your Horse a Chance*

Foster, Carol *The Athletic Horse*

Harris, Charles *Fundamentals of Riding*

Horace-Hayes, Capt M *Veterinary Notes for Horse Owners*

Houghton-Brown, J and Powell-Smith, V *Horse and Stable Management*

Hyland, Ann *Foal to Five Years*

Inderwick, Sheila *Lungeing the Horse & Rider*

Langley, Garda *Understanding Horses*

de Nemethy, B *The De Nemethy Method*

Podhajsky, A *The White Stallions of Vienna*

Rose, M *The Horseman's Notebook*

Swift, S *Centred Riding*

Wathen, G *Horse Trials*